St Michael

BRITAIN
LAND OF CONTRASTS

St Michael

BRITAIN
LAND OF CONTRASTS

EDMUND
SWINGLEHURST
Foreword by Julian Pettifer

PHOTOGRAPHIC ACKNOWLEDGMENTS

John Bethell 8-9, 10, 11, 13, 15, 16, 17, 18, 19, 21, 22, 25, 26, 27, 28-29, 32, 36, 37 right, 39, 40, 42, 48-49, 50 bottom, 59, 61, 62-63, 64-65, 67, 68 top, 68 bottom, 69, 70, 73 top, 73 bottom, 75, 76 top, 76 bottom, 77, 78, 80-81, 82, 83, 84 top, 84 bottom, 85, 87, 88, 90, 94, 95, 96-97, 100, 101, 102 bottom, 104, 105, 106 top, 107, 108, 109, 110, 111, 112-113, 115, 116, 119 bottom, 121, 122, 123, 124, 125, 129, 134, 136 bottom, 140, 141, 144-145, 146, 149, 156, 159, 160-161, 166, 177, 181, 187, 191, 192-193, 201 top, 202, 233, 234, 235, 236; Marcus Brooke 217, 218; W F Davidson 23, 24, 45, 46, 74, 91, 131, 135, 153, 167 top, 168 top, 168 bottom, 169, 170, 171, 173, 182, 183, 185, 196, 204-205; Fotobank 47, 98-99, 186; Robert Harding Picture Library 71; Peter Loughran 60; The Photo Source titlespread, 30-31, 33, 34, 37 left, 41, 43, 44, 50 top, 51, 52, 53, 55 top, 57, 58, 102 top, 103, 106 bottom, 117, 118, 119 top, 120, 126-127, 130, 132-133, 136 top, 137, 138, 139, 147, 148 top, 148 bottom, 150, 151, 152, 154, 155, 157, 158, 162, 163, 164 top, 164 bottom, 167 bottom, 174-175, 176, 179, 180, 184, 188, 189, 195, 198, 199, 201 bottom, 203, 207, 208, 209, 211, 213, 214, 216, 219, 220-221, 223, 224, 226, 227, 229 top, 229 bottom, 230, 231; Edmund Swinglehurst 79; Tony Taylor 89, 92 top, 92 bottom; Judy Todd 56, 143; Wilf Woodhead 55 bottom

Front jacket
Main photograph: Hurstmonceux Castle, Sussex (The Photo Source)
Inset left: Ackworth Colliery, West Yorkshire (ZEFA Picture Library (UK) Limited)
Inset centre: Ben Nevis from Torlundy, Inverness-shire, Scotland (The Photo Source)
Inset right: Lord Mayor's Show, London (The Photo Source)
Back jacket
Stratford-on-Avon, Warwickshire (J. Bethell Photography)
Titlespread
River Wey at Godalming, Surrey (The Photo Source)

Published in 1986 for
Marks and Spencer p.l.c., Baker Street, London
by
The Hamlyn Publishing Group Limited
London · New York · Sydney · Toronto
Bridge House, Twickenham, Middlesex TW1 3SB, England

Foreword copyright © Julian Pettifer 1986
Text and illustrations copyright © 1986
The Hamlyn Publishing Group Limited

ISBN 0 603 03905 7

Printed in Spain

CONTENTS

The British Isles
Counties and Regions

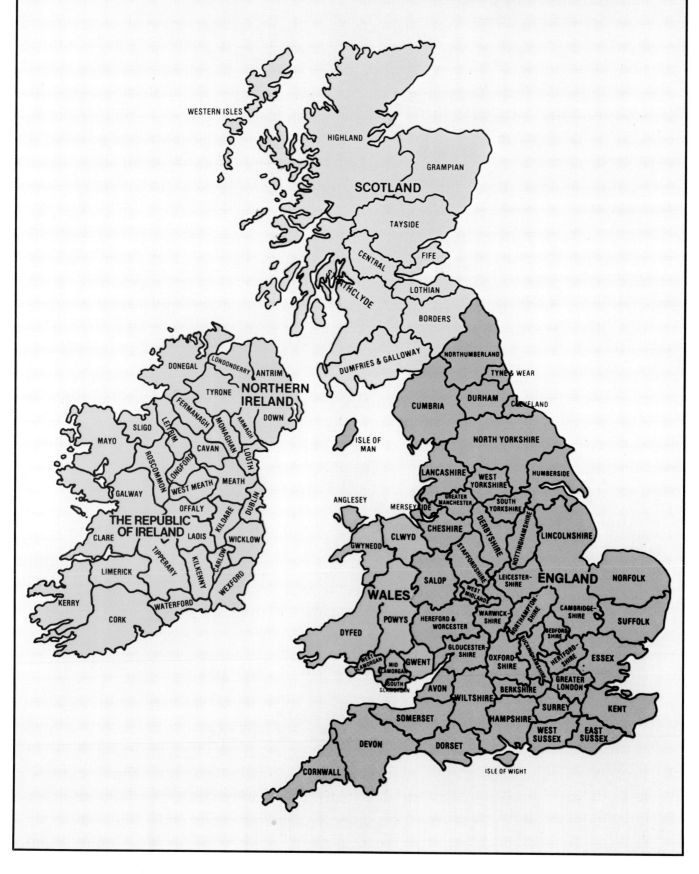

FOREWORD

Recently, whilst working on a natural history of Britain and Ireland for television, a colleague drew my attention to an historical connection I had never made. He pointed out that ten thousand years ago, at about the same period the men of Jericho were building their famous walls for the first time, the last Ice Age was ending in what we now know as the British Isles. After thirteen thousand years buried under an ice-cap up to a mile thick, the landscape was beginning to reappear, virtually lifeless, barren and uninviting.

Now skip forward in time another thousand years to the period when in the Near East there were already cities and city states and when men were already writing on clay tablets and riding in wheeled chariots, and what do you find in Britain? By then, the empty landscapes had been invaded and occupied by trees and had become a great forest where bears and wolves roamed and where our Stone-Age ancestors were just starting to make their first tentative marks upon the land.

Today, the uniformity of that tree-clad terrain has been utterly destroyed and the British Isles display a greater diversity of scenery and of wildlife than almost any other corner of the globe of comparable size. In what amounts to a microsecond of geological time, man has transformed the wilderness and made of it something that is entirely his own. Even the heaths and moors – those remaining parts of Britain we think of as truly wild – are landscapes born of fire, fire which was kindled by man when he began to clear the primeval forest. Where the land was poor, this clearance prepared the way for heath and moor; where the land was good, man planted his crops and grazed his animals and began to create that patchwork of arable and pasture we now regard as typically English.

Visitors to Britain are often surprised to discover that despite our population density, these islands feel remarkably uncrowded. Even in our largest cities we are fortunate to have great green oases, sprawling areas of parkland where we can escape the stress of city life. What is more, despite industrialization and urbanization, our wildlife has adapted remarkably well to change, and in many cases is flourishing in the most unlikely settings. In the canals of Birmingham, kingfishers are found; kestrels are almost commonplace as they soar among the concrete towers of the City of London; and in suburban gardens, early risers frequently find foxes patrolling their lawns.

Britain's gardens are a story and a study in themselves; between them they cover more than a million acres, a greater area than all the national nature reserves put together, and in them can be found an almost incredible range of flora and fauna. Blessed with a benign maritime climate and plentiful rainfall, Britain's gardens are able to nurture trees, shrubs and flowers from all parts of the world. Even in the most modest garden can be found migrants from the Himalayas, the Andes, the Rockies and the Antipodes; while in the gardens of great houses are some of the most extensive plant collections to be found anywhere on earth. British weather, much maligned, is just one factor that gives these islands their astonishing diversity.

To describe Britain as a land of contrasts is to understate the case; it is a land where the terrain, the architecture, the flora and fauna, the physical type of the people and even the language or dialect they speak, can change several times during a half-day's drive.

Consider a journey that starts in, say, Cirencester in Gloucestershire, and meanders south and west and finally crosses the Severn into Wales. We set out from an ancient Roman settlement that became a rich, mediaeval market town with buildings of Cotswold stone; our route progresses south through downland littered with sheep and sarsen stones and with ancient and mysterious prehistoric sites, like Avebury and Silbury Hill; then leaving behind the flint and thatch villages and the chalk streams of Wiltshire, the old coaching road dives down into the 18th-century elegance of Bath.

Just a little further on, the bustling prosperity of the port of Bristol brings us vivid reminders of the slave trade, of the wine business and of the Great Western Railway. At the end of our journey, across the Severn Bridge, we find in Wales a different culture and a different language and we have still reached it in time for tea!

This is why the invitation offered by this book to discover this 'land of contrasts' is so enticing: because in the streets and lanes, in the moors and heathland, on the coasts and in the estuaries, can be read the history of man in these islands. In order to read and understand that history, one must first know the alphabet, and that is what this volume provides: for questing travellers, whether in an armchair or in a vehicle, it is an A.B.C. that will enable them to find those 'tongues in trees, books in the running brooks, sermons in stones and good in everything'.

Boxford, Berkshire 1986

THE TOWN
─── AND ───
COUNTRY CITY

No other capital city in the world has the good fortune to possess open spaces to match those in London. For this Londoners must thank the landed gentry who once owned large estates around their London homes and who, when the time came to join the wave of developers in the eighteenth and nineteenth centuries, preserved parks and squares to remind them of the countryside they were losing. Some of the great London parks were once hunting preserves for Tudor monarchs; other green areas, like Berkeley Square, were part of the estates of dukes. Today these open spaces give the metropolis a touch of the country.

Stroll in St. James's Park in the springtime and see the crocus bursting gaily through the grass and the cascades of new green leaves on the willows. Row on the Long Water in Kensington, or ride in Rotten Row on a misty morning, and you could be miles away from the towering hotels of Park Lane. Further from the centre, in Hampstead or Richmond, great stretches of true countryside have been preserved; and along the riverside there are constant reminders that, until a couple of centuries ago, London was little bigger than a modern country town.

In many built-up areas of London some of the feeling of country remains. There are the small terraced houses and mews cottages, once built for working folk but now highly prized by those who can afford them. Chelsea is full of streets of these delightful eighteenth-century buildings – shining with fresh paint or pastel-coloured stucco. Some lovely old cottages and houses can be found in the old villages of Hampstead and Highgate, which were separate from the metropolis until the mid-1800s, but are now surrounded by the developments of the late Victorian and Edwardian eras and the flimsy architecture of the period between the wars.

Contrast and paradox are very much a part of the character of London. To begin with, the centre of the metropolis is actually two cities, the City of London and the City of Westminster, each with their own clearly defined characters. The City of London is

Charles II once enjoyed royal picnics and kept an ice cellar in Green Park, one of the chain of parks which runs through the West End of London from Kensington Palace to Whitehall. The park was created in 1668.

the financial centre and is known as 'The City', which tells you something about its confidence in itself. The City has always been (and still is, though some would like to think otherwise) a male domain – a place where men adopt the uniform of dark suit in order to prevent their personalities from intruding in the business of the market-place. The City has been a place of business since Roman times. The people who work there are concerned with the serious side of life: the borrowing and lending of money, interest rates, taking risks and insuring against the consequences, all the essential activities without which the more frivolous ventures of London's West End could not exist.

In the West End the projection of personality is part of the strategy of the kinds of business the City of Westminster is engaged in, whether it is politics or shopkeeping. The people in the streets – and here at least half of them are women – are fashionably and colourfully dressed. Unlike the more traditional haunts in the City, the pubs, restaurants and wine bars of the West End attract custom as much by their appearance and character as by the food and drink they serve, and are as subject to changing fashions as the length of a skirt.

The characters of the different pieces of London's jigsaw have been formed over the centuries and their origins have been obscured by the passing of time. How many people know that St. James became an area of social clubs in the time of Charles II, or

In Oxford Street big stores, cut-price shops, fruit stalls and street vendors compete to capture the attention of shoppers.

At the boundary of the City of Westminster and the City of London stands the Temple Bar Memorial erected in 1880. Towering behind it are the imposing neo-Gothic Royal Courts of Justice.

that raffish Leicester Square was the centre of London prostitution in the nineteenth century, or that Chelsea was the Bohemia of the Victorian age? The many aspects to London's personality provide an endless source of fascination to anyone interested in the evolution of society. This interest does not lie in the centre alone; Hampstead, Islington, Hackney, Dulwich and Crystal Palace, not to mention Battersea, Chelsea, Fulham and Ealing, are all different worlds within the London universe.

The City

As you drive along the Strand into the City you will be watched by a griffin. The mythical monster with the head of an eagle and the body of a lion is the symbol of the City and it stands on a pedestal at the entrance to Fleet Street. On this spot once stood a city gate with iron railings where the heads of criminals and political enemies were impaled. The gate (removed in 1878 to Theobalds Park, Hertfordshire) was known as the Temple Bar and stood in the midst of an area inhabited by lawyers. Within sight is the fine church of St. Clement's Dane on its little green island in the Strand. This is overlooked by a huge Gothic-style building which houses the Royal Courts of Justice, commonly known as the Law Courts, opened by Queen Victoria in 1882. The courts have public galleries where the general public can observe the dramas that take place in the courtrooms.

The Law Courts are the centre of an extensive area occupied by the Inns of Court which combine the characteristics of the medieval guilds with those of a modern university. To the north of the Law Courts lie Lincoln's Inn Fields, named after the Earl of Lincoln who founded a law school in the fifteenth century, and Gray's Inn, a fourteenth-century law school. The Great Hall of Gray's Inn was damaged during the Second World War, but has been restored thanks to the generosity of the American Bar Association. To the south of Temple Bar lie the Inner and Middle Temple, two great Inns of Court centred on the Temple Church, a twelfth-century building with many stone carvings of crusaders of the Order of the Knights Templar, who made this their headquarters. The Knights Templar allowed students to read law in the Temple. When the Templars were suppressed in 1312 the students continued to use the Temple, gradually making it their own. The Temple precincts, with their eighteenth- and nineteenth-century houses and their lawns and trees, are one of the most beautiful parts of central London and retain the calm, unhurried air of the days when Dr. Johnson strolled through them on his way to his house in Gough Square, to the north of Fleet Street.

The contrast between the quiet haven of the law and the maelstrom of the media is marked. Fleet Street is usually crowded with traffic and the narrow streets nearby are jammed with giant lorries delivering rolls of newsprint to the voracious presses. The first daily newspaper was printed in Fleet Street in 1702 and Britain's national newspapers have been produced there ever since. Today, however, crises in the newspaper industry have led to some moves to new printing and newspaper offices in London's East End.

At the west end of Fleet Street, where the 1666 Fire of London died out, you can still see two pre-Fire timbered buildings. One is The Wig and Pen Club and the other Prince Henry's Room, named after the eldest son of James I who died in 1612. Opposite is the church of St. Dunstan-in-the-West, which has a statue of Queen Elizabeth I that was made during her lifetime on its façade. Further down Fleet Street, on the left, is the Old Cheshire Cheese. Built in 1667, this was a haunt of Dr. Johnson, James Boswell and Oliver Goldsmith. Off to the right is St. Bride's, one of the most attractive of the Wren city churches, with an exceptionally beautiful spire. Samuel Pepys was baptized here and Samuel Richardson and Richard Lovelace, the Cavalier poet, were buried here.

At its eastern end Fleet Street slopes down to Ludgate Circus and what used to be the valley of the Fleet River, which now runs under the road. On the east bank of the river is Ludgate Hill, which leads up to St. Paul's. St. Paul's is a masterpiece of English architecture. Wren's finest achievement in the construction of the cathedral was the erection of the dome for which he had to invent a

St. Paul's Cathedral was built by Sir Christopher Wren to replace the old cathedral which was burnt down during the Great Fire of London in 1666. Work on St. Paul's began in 1675 and was completed in 1697.

double shell in order to support the stone lantern above. There are 727 steps from the floor of the cathedral to the ball above the lantern and, on the way up, you can enjoy magnificent views of London from the Stone Gallery below the dome and the Golden Gallery above it. The body of the church contains numerous monuments to famous men including one to Wellington and another to Nelson. By the choir stands the shrouded figure of one of England's greatest poets, John Donne, who was once Dean of St. Paul's. In the crypt there are more monuments and tombs including those of many famous painters such as Turner, Reynolds and Van Dyck.

To the east of St. Paul's the city planners have had the good sense to leave enough open spaces for the beauty of the cathedral to be appreciated. There are glorious views from St. Paul's Churchyard and New Change. Beyond New Change is Watling Street, under which lies the road the Romans built. More visible evidence of Roman London can be found at Queen Victoria Street, where the excavated Temple of Mithras was re-erected. Near the temple is St. Stephen Walbrook, another fine Wren church, which possesses much of its original furniture.

The Mansion House, home of the Lord Mayor of London, with its great portico of Corinthian columns, stands between the church and the Bank. Known simply as Bank, this open square has the Bank of England rising up on one side. In the paved centre of the square you will see another Corinthian portico, that of the Royal Exchange, adding to the Roman forum atmosphere of the City centre. Bank is the meeting point for a number of important City streets. Queen Elizabeth Street enters from the west, as does Poultry, leading to Cheapside on which lies St. Mary-le-Bow. It is said that only if you were born within hearing distance of this church's famous 'Bow bells' are you a true Londoner. To the north, along the west side of the Bank of England, is Prince's Street, leading to Gresham Street and the Guildhall. Originally built in the fifteenth century and twice rebuilt – after the Great Fire in 1666 and after the Second World War – the Guildhall is the City of London's Hall, where the Court of Common Council that governs the City meets.

To the east of Bank are Cornhill and narrow Threadneadle Street, at the end of which rises the eye-catching National Westminster Bank tower and the new Stock Exchange building. To the south is King William Street, with the church of St. Mary Woolnoth on the corner of Lombard Street. King William Street leads down to London Bridge and the Monument, which marks the spot where the Fire of London began. Wren designed this giant Doric column to provide a fine viewing platform for those prepared to mount the 311 steps of the spiral staircase to the top. The Monument stands on Fish Hill Street, named because of its proximity to Billingsgate – once London's greatest fish market and, before that, the site of the Roman port. During recent excavations for the foundations of a new office block the quaysides of the port were discovered along Lower Thames Street, which is also the site of a fine Wren church, St. Magnus the Martyr.

Beyond Billingsgate Lower Thames Street rises to Tower Hill. This is overlooked by All Hallows Church, from whose tower Pepys watched the Fire of London. The church has been much damaged by war but still contains some fragments of its Saxon origins and, in the undercroft, there are Roman remains and burnt-out fragments of the London to which Boadicea set fire in the first century BC. A small section of Roman wall stands in a green space in front of the Port of London Authority building which overlooks the Tower of London.

The Tower of London, a fortress by the Thames, has a central white tower which was erected by William the Conqueror. The outer walls and towers were added later. Over the centuries the Tower has been the home of English monarchs, a prison for political prisoners, an arsenal, the Mint, Public Records Office and Royal Observatory. Today it is a fascinating museum of English history where you can walk in the footsteps of powerful kings and the unhappy victims of their anger, like Anne Boleyn; of failed conspirators like Lady Jane Grey, queen for just nine days; and of the murdered Princes, sons of Edward IV, supposedly killed by Richard III. A grim but fascinating story unfolds within these walls which, legend has it, will stand until the ravens that strut on Tower Green, once the site of the executioner's block, have flown away.

Tower Bridge, looming over the Thames by the Tower, was built in the late 1800s. Its drawbridge used to open and close to allow the passage of ships from America, Asia and Africa into the Pool of London. Now, however, the Port of London no longer exists. Instead, St. Katherine's Dock is a marina with a leisure area of pubs, shops and museums, with famous old Thames vessels moored along the quays. Beyond is a wilderness of empty sites and silent docks waiting for the developers.

In Tudor times the South Bank was the leisure area of London town. There were theatres like The Globe, where William

The White Tower, the oldest part of the famous Tower of London was built by William the Conqueror. Henry III and Edward I added the outer defences.

Shakespeare's plays were performed. There were drinking houses, bear pits, gardens and brothels, frowned on by city businessmen but supported by Tudor monarchs. But as the colonial empire grew, this bank of the Thames became a place of warehouses where products from all over the world were unloaded and stored. All that remains of the turbulent Elizabethan quarter is the medieval church of Southwark where Shakespeare's brother Edmund is buried and John Harvard, founder of Harvard University, was baptized.

If you retrace your steps across London Bridge and head up Gracechurch Street to Bishopsgate you will be surprised, if it

Once part of the busy Port of London, St. Katharine's dock is now a leisure area with hotels, shops and restaurants.

The Romans had a lookout tower where the modern Barbican rises in the City of London. This residential and artistic complex is the home of the Royal Shakespeare Company and the London Symphony Orchestra.

happens to be a Sunday, to find a scene of weekday bustle; shops open, streets filled with market stalls and the raucous cries of traders encouraging throngs of bystanders to buy their wares. This is because traditionally this is a Jewish area, and for Jews Sunday is a day of business. Long known as Petticoat Lane Market (though most of it takes place in Middlesex Street) this part of London has become a Sunday showplace crowded with people looking for a bargain or simply enjoying the show – getting their picture taken with a live monkey or snake, or succumbing to the trader's offer of three hand-embroidered T-shirts for the price of one.

Leaving this delightful fairground and crossing Bishopsgate you will find Wormwood Street which will lead you to London Wall. This is where the old city wall ran in Roman times but there is not much of it left today. The area was bombed flat in the Second World War and has been rebuilt as a mini Manhattan, named the Barbican as a reminder of the Roman Fort which stood at the western end of London Wall. Fragments of the wall remain by the splendid Museum of London, where the history of London is laid out in a well presented exhibition. The Museum is only one part of the large Barbican development which is intended as a residential and leisure area within the City, providing theatres, a concert hall, art galleries, cinemas and halls for exhibitions and conferences.

To the west of the Barbican is Smithfield. The Smithfield meat market trades under a vast wrought-iron and glass palace of

Nelson stands on his column in Trafalgar Square guarded by Landseer's lions and flanked by the statues of military and naval heroes Napier and Havelock.

the 1860s. This was erected on the site used since the Middle Ages for St. Bartholomew's Fair, where cloth and live cattle were sold. Smithfield has also been the site of jousts and tournaments and of executions. William Wallace, leader of the Scots, died there in 1305 and Wat Tyler in 1381. Many victims of religious persecution were burned at the stake in the place which today is filled with carcasses of animals intended for the shops and restaurants of London and the surrounding area. Because of its unusual trading hours – most activity takes place between midnight and morning – many pubs around the market are open outside normal hours and cafés serve some of the best breakfasts in London.

Across the square from the market is St. Bartholomew's Hospital, more familiarly known as Barts. The hospital was founded in 1123 by Rahere, a courtier of Henry I, in gratitude for recovering from a serious illness while in Rome. It adjoined an Augustinian Priory. The Priory's church lies behind a timbered façade on the east side of the square. This is the oldest and in some ways the most impressive church in London. It evokes the earliest years of medieval England with its heavy rounded arches and deeply mystical atmosphere. The part now visible is only the choir of the former church, much of which was destroyed during the dissolution of the monasteries. However, what is left is magnificent, a reminder of the great monasteries from which sprang the learning and culture that helped to build modern Europe.

The western limits of the City of London are in the region of Farringdon Street (under which runs the River Fleet down to Ludgate Circus) then across on the far side you enter the City of Westminster.

The City of Westminster

Unlike the City of London, Westminster has several focal points. There is Whitehall, the home of government; and Piccadilly and Oxford Street, an area of shops and places of entertainment. There is Knightsbridge, the smart shopping area, whose queen is Harrods, and the museum complex of Kensington. Each of these areas reflects a different facet of the City of Westminster.

The government area is contained between Trafalgar and Parliament Squares. Trafalgar Square is dominated by the column from the top of which Nelson stares out towards the Thames and the Channel, and is surrounded by a heterogenous collection of buildings which include the National Gallery and the Wren church of St. Martin in the Fields.

Down Whitehall there is the Horse Guards building, easily identified by the mounted sentries at the gates. Opposite is a fine Inigo Jones building. This is the Banqueting House of the former Whitehall Palace, which burned down in 1698. The paintings on

Though built between 1840 and 1850 by Sir Charles Barry, the new Palace of Westminster, popularly called the Houses of Parliament, conveys a feeling of antiquity.

the ceiling were commissioned by James I and earned Rubens a knighthood from King Charles I, who was beheaded in the same hall in 1649. Whitehall is lined with blocks of government buildings which include the Treasury. In the centre of Whitehall a plain, dignified monolith, the Cenotaph, commemorates the dead of the two World Wars and is the focal point of the Armistice Day remembrance ceremony. Turning off Whitehall, on the right, is Downing Street, home of the Prime Minister.

Parliament Square is one of the most satisfying squares in London. It gathers round it buildings representing the faith, hope and glory of a nation. Faith is represented by the great Abbey of Westminster, now showing its true beauty after centuries of grime have been washed off. The nation's hope is represented by the Palace of Westminster; the oldest part, Westminster Hall, was initiated by William Rufus in the eleventh century, but most of the hall was completed by Richard II. Many of the great events of English history have taken place here; Charles I was condemned to death in Westminster Hall, as were William Wallace, Sir Thomas More and Guy Fawkes. Glory is represented in Old Palace Yard and Parliament Square by the statues of great statesmen and military leaders, among them Richard the Lionheart, Field Marshall Lord Smuts, Lord Palmerston, Disraeli, Abraham Lincoln, George Canning and Sir Winston Churchill.

The present Houses of Parliament are a relatively recent addition. They were built in the nineteenth century in the then popular neo-Gothic style, replacing a previous building burned down in 1834. The Palace of Westminster, so called because a royal palace stood here from the time of Edward the Confessor until Henry VIII moved his residence to Whitehall, has three towers. The Victoria Tower, at the west end, overlooks the Victoria Tower Gardens in which there is a fine copy of the Rodin bronze of the Burghers of Calais. The Palace has a central spire and, of course, the clock tower erroneously called 'Big Ben', after the name of the bell which strikes the hours.

Across the river on the south bank is Lambeth Palace, home of the Archbishop of Canterbury. The entrance, by Mortons Tower, is a red brick gateway built in the fifteenth century. The Great Hall echoes the architecture of Westminster Hall and is now a library open to the public. Inside the precincts of the Palace is a guardroom which houses a collection of paintings of past Archbishops by such painters as Holbein, Van Dyck and Reynolds.

Westminster Bridge is to the north of the Palace. The view from this bridge inspired Wordsworth to write: 'Earth has not anything to show more fair, Dull would he be of soul who could pass by a sight so touching in its majesty.' Since Wordsworth's day much has changed, but the view of the Thames still stirs the blood. If you cross the bridge and head towards the north bank you will see the Palace of Westminster, all pinnacles and towers, and a view which inspired Derain and Monet to produce some of the most colourful pictures of London ever painted. To the north the river sweeps round in a curve along the Victoria Embankment in front of government buildings and the Victorian-Gothic Whitehall complex. Then there is Charing Cross Railway Bridge, new since Wordsworth's day, obscuring the panorama of the City and St. Paul's which is best seen from either Waterloo Bridge or the terraces of the Royal Festival Hall.

The Festival Hall was the first of the pleasure palaces erected on a site formerly covered with warehouses and its name is a

Three auditoria provide spectacular and intimate drama in the National Theatre building on the South Bank of the Thames and from its terraces audiences can enjoy the exciting panorama of the north bank.

reminder of the great Festival of Britain 1951. Since then the leisure and arts complex has been extended by the addition of the Queen Elizabeth Hall, Purcell Room, Hayward Art Gallery, the National Film Theatre and the National Theatre's Olivier, Lyttleton and Cottesloe theatres. The dedication of the South Bank to open spaces and non-commercial buildings is a notable achievement and has restored to London's riverside some of the glory it had in Tudor times, when the Thames was an important waterway along which stood the houses of the most important men in England.

London's Open Spaces

The sense of spaciousness which the river contributes to the city is heightened by its parks and squares – the bits of countryside that have been left behind, containing copses of trees, streams and ponds, and a resident bird and animal population.

Green Park and St. James's Park are good examples. The Tyburn River used to flow through Green Park, where Charles II took his dogs for walks. In St. James's Park the river was damned up to make the present lake on which an island remains, providing a breeding ground for ducks, geese and other waterfowl which frequent the lake and are fed by kindly Londoners and visitors. The

The Victoria Memorial and the façade of Buckingham Palace were designed by
Sir Aston Webb in 1913. Behind them lies the palace created by Nash.

view from the bridge across the lake towards Horse Guards Parade
is one of the most sublime city views in the world, especially when
the guards are on parade, thrilling the international crowds that
gather to watch such spectacles as the changing of the guard at
Buckingham Palace.

The Palace is the focal point of the Mall, the ceremonious
avenue down which Heads of State ride when visiting the British
monarch. It is a pity that this fine building by John Nash (whose
vision of London, if followed, would have left us with the most
imaginative and elegant city on earth) is hidden by the institutional
façade erected in 1913. However the rear of the Palace remains as
Nash designed it and provides an appropriate background to the
Queen's garden parties. In front of the Palace stands a monument
to the most powerful queen of all time, Victoria.

St. James's Palace stands on the site of a leper hospital taken
over by Henry VIII and it still retains the Tudor gatehouse and the
wings designed by Wren for Charles II. It was restored by Nash for
George IV and the unity of the original conception has been
preserved. St. James's, which was used as the Royal Palace after
Whitehall burned down, is still the official name of the British
Royal Court to which all ambassadors are accredited. It has a long
and interesting history. Within its walls were born Mary (wife of
William of Orange), Queen Anne, Charles Stuart (the Old
Pretender), and George IV. Charles I spent his last days here with
his family, before walking across the park to Whitehall for his
execution.

Behind St. James's Palace lies Clarence House, built for the
Duke of Clarence (later William IV) by Nash. Next to it, by Green
Park, is Lancaster House, built by Wyatt for the Duke of York. On
Marlborough Road is the Chapel Royal, built for Henry VIII,
where Gibbons and Purcell were organists, and Marlborough
House, built by Wren for the Duke of Marlborough, who brought

the bricks from France as ballast after his campaigns. At the eastern end of the Mall you can see some more of Nash's work in Carlton House Terrace, a long, rather theatrical structure built in the style of the terraces he built in Regents Park and which he hoped to join to the Mall by a colonnaded Regent Street.

Unlike the East End, where there is a sudden change of atmosphere between the City and the world of small businesses and working class homes, the style of the West End continues from Piccadilly into Knightsbridge. A short bus ride – and about a century – separates the Queen Anne houses of the older part of Mayfair from the nineteenth-century solidity of the Belgravia mansions. Both areas are the products of the well-to-do, able to afford to live in elegant affluence. Knightsbridge and Sloane Street are the local shopping streets and that speaks for itself.

The ornate neo-Gothic memorial to Prince Albert makes a striking companion to the Roman-style Albert Hall at the south of Kensington Gardens.

Hyde Park is the greatest of the London parks. It stretches from Mayfair to Kensington and adjoins Kensington Gardens, the former grounds of Kensington Palace. Linking the parks is the Serpentine, a boating lake in which you can bathe and which provides an attractive foreground to views of Park Lane. To the south of Kensington Gardens are the great museums of London. There is the Victoria and Albert, housed in an Italianate extravaganza topped by an imperial crown, and the Natural History Museum, a neo-Gothic-Romanesque structure, decorated with gargoyles and grotesque animals. The Science Museum and the Geological Museum are more discreet, constructed in the institutional style of the 1920s and 1930s.

More open spaces can be found in north London. There is Regent's Park, formerly a Henry VIII hunting ground; and Hampstead Heath, stretching along a hillside carved by valleys, a string of ponds marking the bed of the River Fleet. You can stroll along Spaniards Way to Dick Turpin's haunt, The Spaniards Inn, and from here and other high points on the Heath enjoy superb views over London.

Adjoining the Heath is Kenwood, home of Lord Iveagh, which has a magnificent wooded garden and a mansion with an outstanding collection of paintings. To the west is Hampstead Village and to the east Highgate, both retaining something of the atmosphere of former times. Constable lived in Hampstead and painted the Heath. Keats lived in Hampstead's Keats Grove, where his house is now a museum. Coleridge is buried at St. Michael's Church in Highgate and Karl Marx, who died in Hampstead, is buried in Highgate's famous cemetery.

From the heights of Hampstead you can look south, over the river, to the corresponding heights of the Crystal Palace, now covered in buildings except for the park. At one time Crystal Palace Hill was also a piece of countryside within the metropolis, but now only a memory of country remains, in Dulwich village,

Regent's Park is one of London's most popular open spaces for it includes Queen Mary's Rose Garden, an open air theatre and London zoo.

whose cottages form a small enclave in the tide of suburbia which engulfed London at the beginning of this century.

Outer London

In Tudor times the growing affluence of England and the strength of the monarchy gave English kings the time and the money to enjoy life outside London. As it no longer became necessary to live in the Tower, monarchs began to look for pleasant places along the river in which to hold their Courts. Among these were Greenwich, Hampton Court and Kew.

Greenwich was the gateway to London and had attracted royal attention since the time of Henry VI, who took an existing palace from Duke Humphrey during the Wars of the Roses. Henry VII re-built the Palace of Pleasance there, renaming it Placentia. Henry VIII was very fond of Greenwich and his daughter Elizabeth was born there. However, when Chancellor Wolsey offered him Hampton Court as a peace offering (for Wolsey had realized that the King resented his ostentatious lifestyle) Henry accepted the offer and moved up river.

*John Keats and Captain Marryat went to school at Enfield and Charles Lamb
and his sister lived in one of these charming cottages in Gentlemen's Row.*

Greenwich still has a royal air and its buildings centre on the
Queen's House, where you can see paintings of England's
triumphs at sea by, among others, the Dutch Van de Velde
painters. The Queen's House and the wings to each side are now
part of the National Maritime Museum. Between here and the
River Thames is the Royal Naval College, a building by
Christopher Wren, who also built the Observatory up on the hill.
Above the buildings stretches Greenwich Park providing views
which, before the industrialization of London's north bank, must
have been full of charm.

The old Royal Observatory built by Wren at Greenwich overlooks other buildings now occupied by the Naval College, the National Maritime Museum and General James Wolfe, hero of Quebec.

Only a few walls remain of Richmond Palace, in Richmond, Surrey, a few miles south-west of London. The Palace is incorporated into houses on Richmond Green. It was a royal manor in the Middle Ages and was rebuilt by Henry VII in 1501. Near it is the Old Deer Park, a royal hunting ground. Beyond you will find Kew Gardens, perhaps the world's most important botanical garden, where the grounds are planted with innumerable species of trees and the giant greenhouses shelter tropical, temperate and desert flora. In the gardens there are lakes, temples, a pagoda and many species of wildfowl.

Across the Thames lies another splendid estate, Syon House, still the home of the Duke of Northumberland, whose family were granted it by Elizabeth I. Not too far away to the north is Osterley, the house of Elizabeth's royal banker, Sir Thomas Gresham. Also nearby, up river from Richmond, is Ham House, home of the Earl of Lauderdale, a friend of Charles II. In later years Ham was owned by the uncle of the poet William Cowper who spent some time there. Ham is on the edge of Richmond Park which was enclosed in 1637 by Charles I. Now herds of deer roam freely in this lovely piece of countryside.

The beautiful riverside of Kew, Richmond, Teddington and Twickenham, where courtiers built their houses well into the nineteenth century, has survived much of the urban development that has overtaken other parts of the Thames. There are still many old houses, timbered pubs and historic churches on the way to Kingston, now a large and busy town. Hampton Court and its park still occupy most of the loop of the river as it flows in from the west and curls northward towards London.

The red brick palace was built in about 1515 for Cardinal Wolsey. It was enlarged by Henry VIII, who put in the Great Hall, Chapel and tennis court, and added to by William and Mary. There

The Royal Borough of Richmond, where Tudor monarchs had their palaces has a fine eighteenth-century bridge by James Paine.

are three main courts in the Palace, the Base Court, the Clock Court (where you can see the astronomical chart over Anne Boleyn's gateway), and the Fountain Court. The building is superb and is crammed with art treasures. It even has a haunted gallery where the unhappy Catherine Howard is said to walk. The gardens, laid out by William III, stretch down to the Thames and are as satisfying to stroll in as the Palace itself. There is the Tudor tennis court, the famous maze which caused so much hilarity to Jerome K. Jerome's *Three Men in a Boat*, and a great vine which has been producing grapes since it was planted in 1768. Sadly, parts of this magnificent palace were badly damaged by fire in spring 1986.

Across the Kingston Road to the north is Bushey Park, which was used by Henry VIII for hunting. Further west is another royal palace, Windsor Castle, which is still in use today. We will be looking at Windsor more closely in the chapter on the Thames Valley.

THE WEST COUNTRY

HIGH MOORS
— AND —
RUGGED COASTS

In the West Country there is an almost perfect blend of sea and land working together in harmonious counterpoint. Great cliffs protect the far west against the encounter with the Atlantic. Rivers water the green valleys of Devon and Somerset, emptying into the English and Bristol Channels, creating harbours and ports such as Plymouth and Bristol. For the holidaymaker the West Country provides the contrasting but complementary playgrounds of magnificent highland moors and beautiful sandy beaches.

You will find a great difference in character between the West Country's north and south coasts. The north coast bears the brunt of the Atlantic Ocean and the dramatic weather it brings to our shores. The Atlantic sweeps past Land's End in an impressive show of strength, crashing its waves against the rocky cliffs and violent winds bend the trees into grotesque shapes. The south coast has its back to the gales. The sea is calm, with sheltered estuaries, and the breeze is balmy, encouraging the growth of palms, oleanders and early spring flowers.

As you move into the interior of the western landmass the character of the landscape softens. Cornwall is rugged and resolute – a land of heaths and stone walls – but not without its softer edges. Wherever there is a sheltered valley or a hidden creek, the temperate conditions encourage the growth of trees and shrubs and early flowers. In Devon there is the sunny southern Riviera and, in contrast, Dartmoor – a hard unforgiving place in bad weather, but when the sun shines a wonderland of spacious views. There are wooded valleys with tumbling streams which water the green edges of the moor before flowing into the Tamar river system to the west and the Teign to the east. The Exe Valley is a world on its own, gathering the waters of the rivers that flow off Exmoor within sight of the Bristol Channel. The River Exe traverses the whole of Devon from north to south through wooded valleys, water meadows and farms, past villages and castles until it arrives at the city of Exeter and moves further on into the English Channel.

Bowerman's Nose is a strangely weathered column of rocks near the delightful village of Manaton on Dartmoor.

From the westernmost part of England at Land's End there is a superb vista of the Atlantic Ocean with the Longships Lighthouse off-shore and the Scilly Isles some 30 miles away.

The North Coast

From Minehead to Land's End there are many features of enduring interest. From the popular resort of Minehead with its fine sandy beach you can follow the rapidly rising coastal path up Porlock Hill – a steep, twisting and demanding walk which can be avoided by taking the toll road on the sea-slope of the hill. You can stop on Porlock Hill to take in the marvellous scene below with the little harbour of Porlock Weir, and far beyond, across the Bristol Channel, the blue mountains of southern Wales. Behind you lie the Brendon Hills, an area visited by Coleridge who was inspired, perhaps by the deep ravines and rushing torrents, to write *Kubla Khan* in his cottage in the Quantock Hills further to the east. The other lake poets were also drawn to this romantic corner of England. Shelley and his new bride, Harriet Westbrook, came to live at Lynton and Wordsworth lived with his sister Dorothy at Nether Stowey, near to Coleridge.

Following Exmoor's steep coastal border to the west you arrive at Lynton, which lies above a steep, wooded gorge, and then Lynmouth which lies below. The two towns are joined by a funicular railway as well as a winding road. From Lynton you can take a road leading to the famous Valley of the Rocks, or you can walk there on an exciting cliff path which you are likely to share with the mountain sheep that graze on the steep cliff edge.

The Valley of the Rocks, with its soaring green sides topped by jagged rocks, leads on to Woody Bay, a great wooded amphitheatre overlooking the sea. From there you can take a toll road to Lee Bay, a village spread along a delightfully green valley which leads to a sandy beach backed by wooded slopes.

Further west lies Combe Martin, a quiet seaside resort today but once a busy silver mining district. The village stretches along a wooded valley and is overlooked by a promontory with the ominous name of the Little Hangman. The towering cliffs lead round to Ilfracombe, which sadly has suffered the fate of many beautiful places by the sea. The town was rapidly developed in the nineteenth century and the slopes of the hills which drop down to the little harbour are stacked with Victorian mansions now turned into hotels or bed and breakfast houses. The harbour which lies at the foot of Lantern Hill is still surrounded by a cluster of small houses and a church. On its seaward side, high on a mound, is the Chapel of St. Nicholas, whose light has been a beacon for sailors for over 600 years. A short distance inland from Ilfracombe is Chambercombe Manor, built on the foundations of a house erected after the Norman Conquest.

From Ilfracombe the coastal path follows the cliffs westward to Morte Point, a promontary owned by the National Trust, from which there are marvellous views across the finest sands in Devon at Woolacombe. This golden beach, preserved from development, is backed by giant sandhills. Along the northern flank is Woolacombe village, with its many hotels, which runs round to Barricane Beach, a famous hunting ground for exotic shells.

After Woolacombe the Devon coast turns sharply south and the level of the cliffs drops as they skirt the great estuary of the Taw River on which the town of Barnstaple stands. Along the shoreline the sands stretch across the Braunton Barrows Nature Reserve, and the army manoeuvres area which was used by the American troops during their preparations for the Normandy Landings in 1945.

In the seventeenth century when the American colonies were being settled and developed, the area around Barnstaple and Bideford, which lies up the River Torridge, was busy with shipbuilding and trading. Today memories of those great days remain in Barnstaple's eighteenth-century Centre, where you can see a fine colonnade known as Queen Anne's Walk and a fourteenth-century chapel which was once the school attended by John Gay, author of *The Beggars Opera*. At Bideford you can visit the long bridge where Sir Richard Grenville's transatlantic ships were

Bideford lies beside the banks of the River Torridge and stretches into the hills. A fifteenth-century bridge joins the two parts of the town.

Clovelly on the rugged North Devon coast is an old fishing village with a steep, cobbled main street that descends to the sixteenth-century harbour.

moored after he received a charter from Elizabeth I giving him authority over the port.

At the meeting point of the Taw and the Torridge is Appledore, a charming fishing and shipbuilding village which, during the reign of Elizabeth I, received the title of 'free port' for its services to England at the time of the Spanish Armada. In this attractive village of narrow streets and painted houses shipbuilding still goes on at the yards which have in recent years produced replicas of Drake's *Golden Hind*, a Viking ship and a Roman galley.

From Appledore the Devon coast swings westward in a long line of cliffs broken by narrow ravines in which villages cling like the limpets on the rocks below. Clovelly is the star attraction, with its whitewashed houses bordering the quaint cobbled streets that lead down to the tiny harbour. No cars are allowed here, so donkeys are used to transport merchandise for the shops and food and drink for the pubs and restaurants. A delightful spot, but crowded in summer, Clovelly is best approached through the Hobby Drive which runs through the cliff-hanging woods from Hobby Lodge. Less crowded is the village of Bucks Mills, perched at the top of a zig-zag incline leading to the rocky beach below. However, parking can be difficult along the narrow road that descends the wooded ravine to the village.

At the western end of the bay that both Barnstaple and Bideford claim as their own is Hartland Point, a great rocky headland jutting pugnaciously into the Atlantic. It was called Promontory of Hercules by the Romans when they first sailed to England in search of tin and china clay. Hartland Point (99 m; 325 ft high) is a magnificent viewpoint from which to enjoy the broad Atlantic swells that sweep up towards the Bristol Channel and crash against the base of the headland in an embroidery of white surf. From here you can see Lundy Island (which can be visited by boat from Ilfracombe). Below the cliffs is the white lighthouse, reached by a long sloping path. The lighthouse has the important task of warning shipping of the dangers of this stretch of coast – dangers which Drake, Raleigh and Hawkins ignored when they combined to build their private harbour to the west of Hartland, where strangely contorted strata of cliffs plunge down towards razor sharp rocks over which the restless sea breaks in a continuous and riveting display.

From Hartland Point the coast continues southward – a wild coast backed by crumbling cliffs. In the days of sail many ships came to grief along this coast, so many in fact that local inhabitants could make a living by plundering wrecked ships. This practice was strongly condemned by Robert Stephen Hawker, poet and Vicar of Morwenstow. His church can still be found in the ravine that leads steeply to the shore. The graveyard is full of victims of the sea.

At Bude the cliffs descend towards a huge stretch of sandy beach, crowded with visitors in the summer and popular with surfers. At high tide you can swim in the seawater pool at the north of the beach. From Summerleaze Beach a canal stretches inland which once ran as far as Launceston but today it is only navigable for a few miles to Helebridge. South of Bude the cliffs rise again, coming to a high point at Crackington Haven where rocky crags more than 122 m (400 ft) tall tower over the sandy beach on which great reefs stretch out to sea, resembling a sleeping dragon. On the southern cliffs there are superb views over the reefs called The Strangles, which have claimed many victims in the past.

At Tintagel the natural drama of the scenery is heightened by the connection with the legend of King Arthur. King Arthur's castle is situated on an island crag connected to the mainland by a narrow bridge. Below the crag the sea froths and rumbles around the entrance to Merlin's cave, which tunnels through the crag from end to end. The scenery is spectacular and, even if the legendary King Arthur was never really here, the setting is perfect for the tales of heroism and magic, first written by Geoffrey de Monmouth in the twelfth century and elaborated by Tennyson in the nineteenth. A genuine historic relic is the fourteenth-century manor now in the care of the National Trust and used as a post office. This building was part of the estate of Tintagel owned by the Black Prince.

Inland from Tintagel is Camelford, which locals claim to be the site of Arthur's Camelot, and old Slaughter Bridge, supposedly the site of the King's last battle. The Camel River flows through Camelford and on down to Padstow, an ancient fishing village where St. Petroc founded a monastery in the sixth century. The fourteenth-century church up above the old port commemorates his name. In the Camel Estuary, north of Padstow, are the little bays of Harbour Cove and Hawkers Cove, which overlook the notorious Doom Bar, a hazard for shipping since the early days of trade with America. Across the harbour is Hayle Bay, a fine sandy beach popular for bathing. Further along the coast to the north lies little Port Isaac. This is a popular spot for tourists, with picturesque whitewashed houses and a busy harbour, crowded with fishing boats and lined with nets.

The lifeboat was once stationed at Padstow but has now been moved to Trevose Head, as silting of the estuary made it difficult

The Gannel is a long narrow inlet once used by shipping but now silted up. It lies to the south of Newquay which has five sandy beaches.

to launch it from the old position. Above the new lighthouse station on 76 m (250 ft) cliffs is a lighthouse which has guided ships safely home since 1842. At Newquay to the south of Trevose Head are some of Cornwall's most famous beaches. Newquay is a large and popular resort and a leading surf centre. The old harbour was once an important fishing port and above it stands Huer's House where a lookout was stationed to watch for signs of shoals of fish out to sea. Since the arrival of the railway in 1875, Newquay has concentrated on becoming a successful seaside resort and, as well as possessing more than six splendid beaches, it provides all kinds of entertainment for its visitors.

There is another good stretch of sand at Perranporth, to the south, ever popular with summer visitors and the surfers who take part in annual surfing championships. An old port, Perranporth used to be called St. Pirans after the saint who was supposed to have sailed from Ireland on a millstone. For some time the church of St. Pirans was completely covered by the shifting sand dunes of Perranporth but it was excavated and restored in 1835. Since then another church has been built at Perranzabuloe further inland.

Originally the villagers of Perranporth depended for their livelihood on tin mining, an industry that flourished all round the Cornish coast and has left its monuments in the distinctively-shaped towers which can be seen today. These towers housed the lifting gear which took miners up and down the mines and some of them had underground corridors which extended right under the sea. At St. Agnes you can see several deserted mines and you can visit the now forgotten port of Trevaunance which was specially built for the loading of tin and copper from the St. Agnes mine.

The final stretch of the north coast of Cornwall begins at the picturesque port of St. Ives which rises in an amphitheatre of white houses above the sands of St. Ives Bay. St. Ives has become a famous gathering place for artists. Whistler, Sickert and, more recently, Nicholson and Barbara Hepworth have all been residents of St. Ives. Although very popular in the summer because of its fine beaches, St. Ives has managed to retain the atmosphere of an old port. The area between the harbour and Porthmeor Beach is especially charming. Porthmeor is the last accessible stretch of sand before Land's End as, from here, sheer granite cliffs descend vertically to the sea.

On the way to Land's End are Zennor Head and the village of Zennor. There is a legend that the Squire of Zennor was seduced by a mermaid and you can find her carved effigy on one of the pews in the church. D. H. Lawrence lived at Zennor during the First World War but was ordered to leave as the locals thought his German wife, Frieda, was signalling to German submarines at sea.

As you follow the Cornish coast southward you will come to Cape Cornwall. This is a promontory which, though not the farthest western point of England, has a wilder and more solitary grandeur than Land's End and is to be recommended to those who like to enjoy nature's wonders without crowds.

Below left: The delightful Cornish harbour of St. Ives was once a busy centre of pilchard fishing but gradually became an artists' haven and a popular summer holiday resort.

Below right: Tin mining has been a Cornish industry since Roman times but now practically all the mines are closed and their engine houses stand empty and in ruins.

The South Coast

The marvellous south-facing coast of the Penwith peninsula is only accessible by walking along the coastal footpath. Do make the effort, as the scenery is breathtaking. There are villages along the way which can be reached by car from the B3315, but the full beauty of the coastline can only be appreciated on foot. From Land's End the coast road heads south past Mill Bay, where imposing cliffs surround a small beach, then on to Gwennap Head, where there is a coastguard station. Ten minutes walk away is Porthgwarra (which can also be reached by road from the B3315). A handful of cottages along the lane leads to the slipway used by fishermen to draw their boats up beyond reach of the tide.

A very short walk along the cliffs to the east brings you to Porthcurno (which can also be reached by road from the B3315). Here you can see the unusual Minack Theatre – a theatre carved out of the cliffs where, in summer, performances are given against a backcloth of sea and sky that the Greeks would have envied. Across the bay you can see another promontory, Tieryn Dinas, on which is situated the tiny village of Treen. Visit the excellent pub there and then take a short walk to see the Logan Stone, a rock precariously balanced on a stack which moves when touched. Dislodging it may prove a costly affair, as Lieutenant Goldsmith discovered in 1824. He moved the stone and was obliged to restore it to its former spot, having had to hire expensive lifting equipment to do so!

From the Logan Stone a short walk across the heather and bracken of the clifftop brings you to a view of Penberth Cove, seen below in the next ravine. Penberth is typical of the tiny Cornish fishing villages which used to be found in every cove along the coast. Between Penberth and Lamorna Cove the road (B3315) takes you inland past a group of stones which, according to legend, were a band of merry maidens turned to stone by a local wizard.

A pleasant wooded lane leads down to Lamorna, past the Wink pub where a nod was as good as a wink if you wanted some of the landlord's contraband brandy. Like many of the little ports along this rugged coast, Lamorna was created for reasons of trade, in this case, granite. A breakwater was built, a few houses sprung up around it and business was brisk for a while. Today, however, Lamorna is simply a beauty spot.

From Lamorna the coast path curls northward along the cliffs to Mousehole, which can also be reached from the B3315. Mousehole and its larger neighbour, Newlyn, used to be artists' haunts some years ago. There are still art galleries in both villages where you can buy paintings of local beauty spots. Near Mousehole is Penlee Point. The lifeboat *Solomon Browne* set off from here in 1981 to rescue a ship in trouble off the coast and was lost with all hands – a tragic event which brought to the public attention the work of generations of lifeboatmen.

Today Newlyn is almost a suburb of Penzance, whose sands stretch along the edge of Mount's Bay. Once a major harbour for the far west of Cornwall, Penzance is now primarily a holiday resort and the embarcation point for the Isles of Scilly. As well as the usual resort entertainments, Penzance has a Museum of Nautical Arts and an Antiquarian Museum. One of the best features of the town is the sandy beach that stretches west to St. Michael's Mount. This conical island is topped by a fourteenth-century castle built on the site of the Benedictine Abbey founded

Penzance in Mount's Bay is renowned for its mild climate which encourages early market crops and flowers.

by Edward the Confessor. Like its counterpart off the coast of Normandy, St. Michael's Mount is now a popular tourist attraction. It can only be reached by ferry at high tide, or by walking over the causeway when the tide is low.

Between Penzance and the Lizard Point the coastal path takes you past rocky cliffs and small coves where houses huddle in hollows. There is Prussia Cove, named after the smuggler John Carter (alias the King of Prussia), and Mullion Cove. There are long stretches of sandy beach at Praa Sands and Poldhu Cove. Poldhu is by the Loe Bar, a stretch of shingle which blocks the entrance to the River Cober, causing it to form a lake just outside Helston. An attractive old stannary town, Helston was the place where the quality of the tin dug up from Cornish mines was assayed. Today it is crowded in summer, with visitors stopping for refreshments or poring over the items in the town's many antique shops.

The Lizard, the southernmost of the two westward-facing Cornish promontories, is a strange and eerie place with tiny, rather austere villages tucked into crevices in its rugged coast and a great central heath, the Goonhilly Downs, on which sit giant aerial dishes relaying messages to satellites 22,000 miles away in space. It is a place of narrow lanes bordered by stone walls; of villages where the graveyards are filled with the victims of the dreaded Manacles Reef near St. Keverne. The only local industry is the polishing of delicately veined serpentine rock from which jewellery and ornaments are made. The Lizard is a totally unspoilt place offering wonderful views and where, in summer, the clifftops are covered with wildflowers, some of which cannot be found anywhere else in Britain.

After the wild spaciousness of the Lizard, Helford Creek comes as a surprise. In this sheltered creek the warm air of southwest England has encouraged the growth of luxuriant vegetation – flowering trees, rhododendrons and hydrangeas flourish here. Along the banks of the Helford River there are small and ancient villages where little sailing boats ride at anchor. Halfway up the river is Helford itself and a ferry which has been in operation since the Middle Ages. Next to Helford is Frenchman's Creek, the location and name of one of Daphne du Maurier's most famous novels. At the upper end of the river is Gweek – a seal sanctuary, where seals stranded on the Cornish coast are cared for until they are able to fend for themselves again.

The south coast of Cornwall and Devon is renowned for its large ports which flourished in the early days of commercial voyages to the New World. First among these was Falmouth, whose wide estuary gave shelter to transatlantic shipping for some 200 years. Falmouth was the first and last port of call for ships leaving Britain and played a crucial role in the success or failure of the commercial ventures in which ships were engaged. From here

The monastery on St. Michael's Mount, like its French counterpart in Normandy, was inspired by St. Michael. The religious building was turned into a castle by the St. Aubyn family and is now owned by the National Trust.

Polperro which is picturesquely packed into a narrow rocky ravine was once a fishing village but has become a very popular seaside showplace.

samples of goods could be sent overland to the London market before the ship arrived in the Capital and important messages could be relayed to the captains before they set sail for America. The captains of Falmouth packets were famous for their seamanship and daring and it is said that their ghosts still swagger along the empty quaysides. These brave men are commemorated in a monument at the Moor, a square in the town centre, and in the Maritime Museum, which has exhibitions of this exciting chapter in Britain's maritime history.

The whole of the Falmouth estuary, known as the Carrick Roads, is a beautiful area with green hills surrounding the broad expanse of water. St. Mawes is a delightful resort; its harbour packed with small boats. Restronquet Creek, on the west side, is famous for its Pandora Inn, named by the captain of the ship sent to capture the *Bounty* mutineers. King Harry's Ferry is where General Eisenhower stayed while preparing the Normandy invasion. At the upper end of the Fal and Truro Rivers is the Cathedral city of Truro.

Between Falmouth and Plymouth, on the borders of Devon, is Cornwall's most visited stretch of coast. There is St. Austell, the centre of the china clay industry where, on the inland skyline, great white conical mounds of china clay rise among the green hills. There are the charming old fishing villages of Fowey, Polperro, Mevagissey and Looe where, although the streets are crowded in summer, a walk on the cliffs can still offer a solitary grandeur which most people miss.

Plymouth and its Sound, into which flows the River Tamar, is perhaps the most historic seaport in the world. Sadly, Plymouth's port suffered severe damage in the Second World War. However, in the Barbican area around Sutton Harbour you can get a glimpse of the Plymouth of Drake and Frobisher; of the Pilgrim Fathers, who founded a new world across the Atlantic, and of James Cook, who sailed from here on his voyage of discovery in the Pacific. Overlooking the Sound is the Citadel, built in the seventeenth century to repel enemies who might try to attack England's growing fleet. In the centre of the Sound is Drake Island, another fortified stronghold, today used as a youth adventure centre. The Hoe, where Drake played his famous game of bowls is still there, with Smeaton's Tower, the top half of the old Eddystone Lighthouse, rising out of it where a warning beacon used to stand.

The south coast of Devon is softer and more rural than the Cornish coast. The land slopes gently down to the sea – a chequerboard of fields where cows graze on the rich pasture. Long estuaries penetrate farmlands and provide sheltered waters for amateur sailors. There are also several large resorts with a good range of hotels and entertainments for the crowds that arrive in the holiday season to enjoy the sunshine of the English Riviera.

Travelling east of Plymouth you will find the coastline dipping southwards towards Bolt Head and Prawle Point. These two headlands form the gateway to the Salcombe Estuary – a beautiful stretch of water surrounded by green trees and gentle hills. At its mouth lies Salcombe, where the buildings make an old-world backdrop to the modern life of the village where people who like to mess about in boats gather in the summer. At the northern end of the estuary is Kingsbridge, another popular boating centre. Within easy reach by car is Dartmouth, one of the most attractive riverside towns in Devon and where the Britannia

Isambard Kingdom Brunel, the famous engineer, built the Royal Albert Bridge over the River Tamar, the border between Devon and Cornwall.

Dartmouth lies on the pretty estuary of the River Dart which has green hills and a narrow sea entrance protected by Tudor castles.

Royal Naval College continues to educate the officers of Britain's Navy. The town has all the charm of a place that has grown over the years, acquiring the character of those who have lived and worked in it.

Dartmouth Estuary, guarded by two castles on its narrow exit to the sea, is a place where beauty and history compete. Used as a congregating point for the Crusaders as early as the twelfth century, the estuary has also seen the fleets of Henry V, the Pilgrim Fathers and the Allied invasion force sheltering in its waters. The estuary is surrounded by magnificent scenery, with steeply rising wooded hills to each side at its southern end, and green fields and hedgerows towards the northern end.

North of Dartmouth are the sheltered waters of Torbay, around which lie Britain's most visited resorts. To the south is Brixham, a busy and extensively developed fishing port which, in its harbour area at least, manages to retain its traditional character, with trawlers moored along the quayside and the replica of the *Golden Hind* floating by the old Market House which houses the British Fisheries Museum.

Next-door neighbour to Brixham is Paignton, a highly developed modern beach resort with plentiful sands, a pier and a modern leisure centre. Its seaside promenade circles the bay to Torquay. Once a peaceful place where naval captains and their families spent their holidays, Torquay moved towards becoming England's great West Country resort when Isambard Kingdom

Sidmouth is a beautifully situated resort with elegant Georgian buildings. Tall red cliffs border the beach to the east.

Brunel's Great Western Railway arrived in 1848. Like Paignton, Torquay is principally a modern tourist centre, but relics of an earlier age can still be found among the hotels and apartment houses. One of these is Torre Abbey, built in the twelfth century, converted into a Georgian mansion in the 1800s, and now used as an art gallery. Also of interest is the Spanish Barn in which prisoners were held at the time of the Armada. Further east is one of the most photographed pieces of coast in south Devon. Between Teignmouth and Dawlish the beach is notable for two large stacks of red sandstone named the Parson and the Clerk and for the railway that runs along the seashore.

The mouth of the River Exe, which enters the sea at Exmouth, is flat and marshy and accommodates a successful nature reserve. Waders and seabirds congregate here in large numbers. Scenically, however, it does little to arouse the imagination. But beyond Exmouth, on the eastern side, the Devon coast once again becomes that incomparable landscape that combines soaring cliffs at Sidmouth, the pastoral simplicity of the countryside at Budleigh Salterton and the enchanting world of little villages like Beer, where the setting (old cottages, sea-battered boats, white cliffs, fishermen's bric-a-brac) has changed very little since Jack Rattenbury was a local smuggler in the early nineteenth century.

The West of England – The Moors

The moors of the West Country may not be as extensive as those in other parts of Britain but they each have a distinctive character of their own. Furthest west, Cornwall's Bodmin Moor is bleak and wild, swept by Atlantic gales. Dartmoor is the largest of the three, with valleys through which rivers flow to the great estuaries of the south coast and rocky crags which add sombre drama to the landscape, especially on misty days. Exmoor is the most wooded, with deep valleys where red deer roam and tumbling streams with leaping trout. Although wild and even menacing in their desolate central heights, all these moors have surprisingly gentle fringes where little farms nestle in valleys and villages, flanked by groves of trees, which huddle against the winter gales but erupt in a blaze of colour in spring as the wild flowers come out in every hedgerow and open space.

You can take the A30 through the centre of Bodmin Moor and visit Bolventor, where Daphne du Maurier's Jamaica Inn still stands – no longer frequented by villainous smugglers but by visitors asking the way to Dozmary Pool, where King Arthur cast his sword, Excalibur, into the bottomless lake. You may be disappointed by the pool's featureless setting unless you visit it in the evening, and the black clouds are scudding in against a coppery sky, or the moon has risen on a cloudless night in June. The best parts of Bodmin moor are not by the roadside of course and, if you want to see the real Bodmin, you need to walk from Bolventor north to Brown Willy where, at 419 m (1,375 ft), you will have a magnificent view of Cornwall and its surrounding seas.

On Dartmoor the wildest parts are also away from the two roads that meet at Two Bridges (the A384 and B3212). Unlike

The 300 square miles of Dartmoor, though now crossed by two main roads, still contain remote spots and isolated houses like the one in this picture.

Bodmin, which is a plateau, Dartmoor is hilly, carved by rivers which flow from its highest points at Willhays and Yes Tor; places which are often inaccessible as they are part of an army artillery range. The Tavy, the Teign, the Dart and the Taw all start their journey to the sea in this area.

To the north is Okehampton, a market town where you will see the remains of a castle with a Norman keep. Nearby, on the hills to the south, is an Iron Age hillfort. If you skirt the moor to the west from Okehampton you will arrive at the delightful village of Lydford which has a castle dating back to the twelfth century and a romantic gorge festooned with greenery. Further south is Tavistock, a busy market town with solid Victorian houses. Then there is Buckland Monachorum and its Abbey which was bought by Sir Francis Drake and converted into a mansion. Today it is the Maritime and Folk Museum. From Buckland you can return across the moor to Princetown, where the grim prison that captured the imagination of Conan Doyle and other writers still stands, and travel on to Postbridge, a very pretty spot with a stone clapper bridge across the River Dart.

After Postbridge you can take a right turn for Widecombe-in-the-Moor where Tom Cobleigh and his friends rode the grey mare that took them to the bourne from which no traveller returns. The village is most attractive but often very crowded. However, there is plenty of moor round about if you want to get away from the madding crowd. To the south lies the Abbey of Buckfastleigh, built by Benedictine monks over a period of 30 years and completed in 1938. In the shop there you can buy their honey and home-made liqueurs.

Exmoor is inextricably associated with the story of Lorna Doone, her evil brother Carver Doone, and Jan Ridd who made sure that love triumphed in the end. The novel, written by R. D. Blackmore, was set in the Doone Valley in the north-west corner

Wiveliscombe at the western end of the Vale of Taunton Deane lies in a rural setting to the south-east of wild Exmoor.

The church at Oare near Doone Valley was the location chosen by R.D.
Blackmore for the wedding of Jan Ridd to Lorna Doone at which a revengeful
Carver Doone shot the bride, and was pursued and killed by Ridd.

of Exmoor. Though Brendon village is often crowded with sight-seers, you can walk or ride up the Doone Valley and appreciate why Blackmore was inspired by this part of the country. Over the top of the Doone Valley is the valley of the River Exe which begins its long journey across Devon here among the gorse and bracken, only a few miles from the sea at Lynmouth.

The Exe runs across Exmoor before it heads south and passes through the village of Exford, a centre for stag hunting which also has literary connections. Henry Williamson, a lover of Exmoor Wildlife, wrote about the red deer and otters of this lovely part of Somerset. A narrow road from Exford heads north across the wildest part of Exmoor and up to the heights of Dunkery Beacon (520 m; 1,705 ft), where there are magnificent views across the Bristol Channel and towards Dartmoor to the south-west.

At the eastern edge of the moor, and about two miles from the sea at Minehead, is Exmoor's most beguiling village, Dunster. Built on the slope of a hill on which rises Dunster Castle, Dunster has been the home of members of the Luttrell family since 1376. The fifteenth- to seventeenth-century pub in the High Street is named after them. The castle is now in the care of the National Trust, an organization which we have to thank for the preservation of so much of the coast and moorland of the West Country.

CHALK HILLS
— AND —
FERTILE VALLEYS

The landscape of southern England is largely made up of the great semicircle of hills stretching from western Dorset, across the treeless Salisbury Plain, and merging into the North and South Downs. This great amphitheatre is broken by rivers, some of the prettiest in the country, converging towards the south and emptying into Southampton Water and Poole Bay.

From the west flow the Frome and the Piddle (also called the Trent); from Blackmoor Vale the Stour; and from Salisbury Plain the Wylye and the Hampshire Avon (not to be confused with another southern counties Avon, which rises in the Cotswolds and flows across northern Wiltshire to the Bristol Channel). Rising on the western shoulders of the North Downs, east of Avon, are the Test and the Itchen – both good fishing rivers. Last but by no means least is the Meon, more a stream than a river, that flows through an unspoilt valley that is the quintessence of the beautiful rural southern counties.

Though the Romans set up their camps and founded towns in this part of England, the real settlement of the land took place in Saxon times. It was then that the land was cleared of the forests that had caused Iron Age people to settle on the chalky heights of Salisbury Plain. Vestiges of the Saxon Age remain today and can be seen in the traditionally small size of the farms, in the Saxon churches and at Winchester, capital of the south and at one time of all England. It was here that the first English King was crowned in 827, and Winchester continued to be capital through the reigns of Alfred the Great, Canute and William the Conqueror, who was crowned at Winchester as well as London.

Winchester is the centre of the lovely region loosely referred to as the Hampshire Basin, through which flow the rivers Avon, Test, Itchen and Meon. The town itself is situated on the slopes of a hill above the River Itchen and is dominated by the Norman cathedral. This is not an arresting building from the outside, for it lacks the spire that gives most cathedrals their impressive height. The interior however is full of interest. It has the longest nave in Britain and houses the shrine of St. Swithin, who was originally buried in the church that bears his name. But in 971 he was

The capital of England until Norman times, Winchester has many interesting features, chief of which is the cathedral, which dates back to the eleventh century. It was built on the site of Roman and Saxon temples.

transferred to Winchester after forty days' delay owing to heavy rain – thus giving rise to the St. Swithin's Day legend. Also buried in the cathedral are William Rufus, who was mysteriously killed while out hunting in the New Forest; Izaak Walton, who loved to fish in the Hampshire rivers; and Jane Austen, the novelist. Outside the Close, in College Street, is the house in which Jane Austen died and, nearby, the gateway to Winchester College, the first of the British public schools, founded by William of Wykeham in 1382. Nearer the river are the ruins of Wolvesey Castle, which dates back to 1129 when Henry of Blois began its construction; nearby is a river walk along the old city walls.

Below: The River Test is one of the great trout fishing rivers of Hampshire and wends its way past idyllic tree-hung banks to Southampton.

Bottom: Though the old harbour was badly damaged during the Second World War something of the old sea-going atmosphere of Nelson's time still remains at Portsmouth.

The great seaport of Southampton, favoured by its double tide has been an important harbour since Roman times.

Winchester is an excellent centre from which to explore Hampshire. To the north-east the land rises into wooded hills nestling among which is Selborne. This is an idyllic place where Gilbert White was inspired to write *A Natural History of Selborne*, which has become a classic among books about country life. The village has hardly changed since White's day and the zig-zag stairway through a hanging wood which he helped to make is still there. Selborne's museum is worth a visit with its exhibits commemorating the career of Captain Oates. Near Selborne is Chawton, a pilgrimage spot for admirers of Jane Austen. The author lived here in a pretty red brick house where you can see her room, her writing implements, clothes and other personal possessions.

From Selborne you can travel south to Petersfield and the Meon Valley. You will pass Droxford with its Saxon church and a detour will take you to Hambledon, a village which claims to be the birthplace of the game of cricket and where there is a well-known vineyard.

What Portsmouth is to the Navy, Southampton is to merchant shipping, though its days of glory when ocean liners competing for Blue Ribands lined its quaysides and celebrities boarded the boat-trains for London are gone forever. However, there is still a good deal of port activity, with Channel ferries crossing to and from France and giant oil tankers putting in at the refineries at Fawley, on Southampton Water.

The commercial aspects of the coast disappear as you leave Southampton Water and turn towards the Solent. Here the creeks and estuaries are crowded with yachts and motor cruisers. At Bucklers Hard on the Beaulieu River they no longer build ships as they did in Nelson's time, but the cottages of the shipbuilders are still there, now turned into hotels and restaurants. Further up the river is Beaulieu Abbey, home of Lord Montague whose interest in old motor cars led him to start a museum which is now considered the best of its kind in Britain. Down the Solent is Lymington, another yachting town and also a ferry embarcation point for the Isle of Wight. The mouth of the River Lymington, like the Avon, helps to water the New Forest.

Although the New Forest is called 'New' it is in fact very old. It was a favourite hunting ground for the Norman kings who imposed severe punishments, including blinding and death, on anyone caught poaching the royal game. In order to increase the size of the forest many Saxon farmers were dispossessed and it is thought that it could have been one of these farmers who killed King William Rufus. The monarchs' privileges lasted into the nineteenth century when they were relinquished. Now the New Forest land and grazing rights are open to all.

Lyndhurst is the New Forest's principal town. It is the seat of the Court of Verderers which concerns itself with preserving the laws and regulations relating to this extensive stretch of woods and heathland. Many animals live in the forest, including red and fallow deer and the New Forest ponies that graze on the commons. Admirers of Lewis Carroll, author of *Alice in Wonderland*, may be interested in visiting the grave of Alice Lidell in Lyndhurst church-yard. She was the original Alice, the inspiration behind one of the most original children's books ever written. Not far to the north, at Minstead, is the grave of Sir Arthur Conan Doyle, creator of Sherlock Holmes.

Of all the rivers of the New Forest it is the Avon that captures the imagination most, for it has some fine stretches of valley and exceptionally pretty villages. In the northern part of the forest it flows through Breamore, a virtually unspoilt Tudor village with a

The New Forest was a Norman hunting ground of woods and heath. William Rufus was killed here by an unknown assassin.

Keats, Longfellow and Swinburne visited the charming Isle of Wight village of
Shanklin around which grew the Victorian seaside resort.

village green surrounded by houses and a manor house which has
been inhabited by the same family, the Hulses, for some 200 years.
Further south it passes through Ringwood, notable for its fine old
houses and trout fishing centre. It was here that the Duke of
Monmouth, illegitimate son of Charles II, was captured after
attempting to wrest the crown from James II.

The Avon enters the sea near Christchurch Harbour, where
it meets up with the Stour. Nearby is a splendid Priory church – a
Norman building with a number of fine features, including a
fifteenth-century tower from which there is an exhilarating view
of the harbour and the promontory of Hengistbury Head beyond.
In the distance you can see the Isle of Wight.

Hardy Country

Dorset lies to the west of the River Avon. Unlike other southern
counties, Dorset has remained outside the main streams of holiday
traffic, a fact that is much appreciated today by the growing
number of people who want to live there. The countryside is
idyllic with rolling hills and wooded valleys and many small
villages where rural life is undisturbed by the passage of heavy
traffic. In Roman times the main routes through Dorset sprang
from Bradbury Rings near Wimborne Minster, which lies a short
distance from the harbours of Poole and Christchurch. You will
not find any Roman remains at Wimborne today but there is a
handsome collegiate church with a red sandstone tower. Like

Blandford Forum to the north, Wimborne is simply a peaceful Dorset town with most of its buildings dating back to the eighteenth century. In Blandford's case the reason for this is that the town was burnt down four times during the sixteenth and seventeenth centuries and very few of the buildings from an earlier date have survived.

West of Blandford Forum is the centre of Thomas Hardy country. The writer was born near Dorchester and he returned there when the novels he had written to remind himself of his home country became successful. The town possesses many relics of the author, including the manuscript of *The Mayor of Casterbridge*, (a non de plume for Dorchester) which is housed at the County Museum. In the museum you can also see some archaeological finds from Roman times but, although Dorchester was once a Roman town, little remains except these relics and a section of wall. Historically Dorchester is remembered as the seat of the Bloody Assizes, when Judge Jeffrey ordered the hanging of 74 of the Duke of Monmouth's supporters and transportation for 175 others.

Hardy Country also stretches to the sea, which is ringed by steep cliffs from Poole to Lyme Regis, providing an exciting walk along the Dorset coast path. Lyme Regis, with its steep High Street, is an unusual and charming seaside resort, its many Regency buildings lending an air of distinction. The town is situated on the slopes of a valley; its houses one above the other, looking out over the Cob. The Cob is a stone pier on which the Duke of Monmouth landed during his ill-advised attempt to oust James II and which has played a role in both Jane Austen's novel *Persuasion* and, more recently, in *The French Lieutenant's Woman* by John Fowles.

Apart from its ability to inspire novelists, Lyme Regis has another interesting aspect; its blue lias cliffs are a fine source of fossils. The largest fossil yet found here is an ichthyosaurus discovered by Mary Anning in 1811. Access to the exposed strata is allowed on payment of a fee.

Westwards the coast rises to Golden Cap and then descends towards Bridport Harbour – once a busy port but now hardly used. From here you can continue east to the Chesil Beach, a bank of pebbles piled up by the sea creating a lagoon, called the Fleet, between sea and shore. Further along the coast is Abbotsbury, a charming village with a fifteenth-century tithe barn and church, all that remain of the monastic estate given away by Henry VIII. Near the village is a swannery of some 4-500 birds. These may be the descendants of the birds raised by the monks for the refectory table. Chesil Beach ends at the Isle of Portland, called the Isle of Slingers by Hardy, which has quarries that have supplied the famous Portland stone to such august buildings as Buckingham Palace and St. Paul's Cathedral. The Isle of Portland juts out to sea and acts as a breakwater to the port of Weymouth, providing safe anchorage for ships. Weymouth, called Budmouth by Hardy, is a fine town with Georgian architecture dating back to when George III visited the town and, by taking his first bathe (to the accompaniment of a chamber orchestra), established Weymouth as a suitable bathing resort.

From Weymouth to the Isle of Purbeck, which protects Poole Harbour from the western gales, the coastline becomes increasingly dramatic as the white chalk hills of Dorset come face to face with the erosive powers of the sea. This is the most spectacular section of the Dorset coast and includes Lulworth

Top: Thomas Hardy, whose source of inspiration was the county of Dorset (renamed Wessex in his novels), was born in this cottage in Higher Bockhampton. The cottage now belongs to the National Trust.

Above: Lulworth Cove is a small bay, almost totally encircled by limestone and oolite cliffs, on the Dorset coast.

Cove, which is almost completely surrounded by cliffs with only a narrow exit to the sea, and the curious perforated rock at Durdle Door. Beyond Lulworth is a no-man's land used by the army as a gunnery range to which entry is not usually permitted. A little further on is another fossil hunters' paradise. The Kimmeridge ledges, like those at Lyme Regis, are a good hunting ground for ammonites, trilobites and other extinct creatures.

The high cliffs come to an end on the Isle of Purbeck after curving past the Tilly Whim Caves to Swanage, a delightful resort which has retained a Victorian atmosphere and possesses two authentic Victorian buildings which once stood in London. One of these is the Wellington Clock Tower, which used to enhance the approach to London Bridge, and the other is the Town Hall, which was originally the Mercers' Hall in Cheapside. Past Swanage is Studland Bay, a wide expanse of sandy beach and a National Nature Reserve. Brownsea Island in the centre of nearby Poole Harbour is another nature reserve where birds of many species breed in safety.

Lady Bankes defied Cromwell's troops from Corfe Castle in 1646 but the Parliamentarians blew it up, reducing it to the picturesque ruins we see today.

Swanage is a fine seaside resort surrounded by cliffs along which there are spectacular walks with fine views of the sea.

Poole is a large industrial town but its old harbour retains the atmosphere of the days when the quaysides were packed with ships taking advantage of the double tide that fills the harbour. Today, however, it is pleasure cruisers and yachts that enjoy this phenomenon. Marinas and boat clubs are plentiful along the front. The Maritime Museum tells the story of Poole's part in the great days of sea voyaging and the famous Poole Pottery works is another interesting place to visit. The town stretches east towards Sandbanks, a residential district with sandy beaches, joining up eventually with Bournemouth, the major seaside resort of the southern counties.

To Hardy, Bournemouth was the resort of Sandbourne, which he likened to a Mediterranean lounging place. Knowing how he loved rural Dorset, it is easy to understand why Hardy sounded disapproving. Bournemouth is still a lounging place, much loved by all who stay there for it provides every form of entertainment likely to be required by the average British family. The beach stretches for miles – all the way to Hengistbury Head. There is a beachside promenade much of the way, past the neighbouring resorts of Boscombe and Southbourne. The cliffs behind the promenade are broken by wooded ravines called chines and

above is a clifftop avenue along which hotels stand shoulder to shoulder among the pines, with their lawns laid out for games of mini golf, bowls or other leisurely activities enjoyed by all ages.

In the centre of the town there is a leisure centre, a concert hall in which the town's own symphony orchestra performs, an art gallery and even a Transport and a Typewriter Museum. In short, Bournemouth is a leisure city by the sea and, if not quite in keeping with the image of Dorset handed down to us by the novels of Thomas Hardy, it nevertheless personifies the new age of prosperity and leisure that his heroes never knew.

Over the Plains and Far Away

The northern area of the southern counties, largely occupied by Wiltshire, is a complete contrast to the areas of the south. You will notice the change in character as you head north from Salisbury. The original town of Salisbury, now known as Old Sarum, was deserted in the twelfth century after the Bishop quarrelled with the military authorities. Old Sarum was then slowly dismantled as the masonry of the houses and cathedral was taken to Salisbury to build the new town. Nevertheless, Old Sarum continued to exist

The mystery of Stonehenge has never been satisfactorily explained but there is little doubt that it represents man's enduring search for an answer to the riddle of the universe.

politically as a 'rotten borough' and sent members to Parliament until 1833 when the whole 'rotten borough' system was exposed. Although today's Salisbury is a bustling market town with a modern shopping precinct, it has preserved the old inns and over-hanging buildings in the old town which was laid out in a grid pattern outside the Cathedral Close.

Salisbury Cathedral is a glorious building which has a unity rare in medieval churches. This is probably due to its rapid erection – 38 years from start to finish – thanks to the energy of Bishop Richard Poore. Even the least architectually-minded passer-by will stop to admire the cathedral's striking exterior, with its 123 m (404 ft) spire. The simplicity of the general design is contrasted by the west front. This was intended to present a dramatic array of sculptures similar to those at Wells Cathedral, but sadly was never completed. The interior is vast and spacious, largely due to the removal of screens and chapels by Wyatt in the eighteenth century. This has produced the same feeling of emptiness as in the great churches of Venice – the Frari and San Zanipolo.

The cathedral contains many features of great interest. The works of the old clock, still ticking away after 700 years, are too large and unusual to miss. Some of the stained glass windows are particularly striking, especially the Tree of Jesse in the south aisle. Among the monuments are the effigies of William Longespee (little known son of Henry II and half-brother to Richard the Lionheart) and Sir John Cheney, a very tall knight who fought at the battle of Bosworth as one of the bodyguards of Henry VII. Other notable parts of the building are the cloisters, entered from the south-west transept, and the Chapter House.

Stonehenge is about 10 miles from Salisbury. Steeped in the history of Iron Age man, in the midst of the large chalky Salisbury

Plain, it is a mysterious monument built some 3,600 years ago. Experts cannot agree on its purpose, some suggest that it was built as a temple, others as a machine for astronomical calculation. There are other mysteries surrounding it too; how, for example, did the blue stones made of a granite found in south Wales arrive at Stonehenge? And is Stonehenge one monument, or three imposed one upon the other? The fascination that the ancient stone circles hold for modern people is evident from the large number who visit, so many in fact that the authorities have now closed off the entrance to the monument itself. It can now only be seen from the outside, much to the chagrin of the Most Ancient Order of Druids who keep a midnight vigil at Stonehenge on Midsummer Day every year.

Stonehenge is not the only stone circle erected by prehistoric man in north Wiltshire; there is another at Avebury, by the Marlborough Downs. The Avebury stones were set up even earlier than the main part of Stonehenge and consist of a circle of stones quarried from the Marlborough Downs with an additional avenue of stones leading south-east to Overton Hill, over a mile away. East of Avebury is the handsome town of Marlborough. It has a wide main street bordered by Georgian buildings, with a church at each end. Contrary to what you might imagine, the

The charming town of Marlborough in Wiltshire has a fine wide colonnaded High Street punctuated at each end by a church.

The River Avon flows through the steep wooded valley in which lies the old stone-built town of Bradford-on-Avon. The bridge was built in the seventeenth-century but contains two thirteenth-century arches.

name of the town does not commemorate the famous eighteenth-century English general, but is derived from the name of a nearby hillock, Maerls Barrow.

The western edge of north Wiltshire lies in the valley of the Bristol Avon, between Salisbury Plain and the Cotswold and Somerset hills. From medieval times up until the 1900s this was a prosperous land peopled by farmers and weavers. Many of the lovely villages and splendid houses we see today were built during that period. Bradford-on-Avon is near the Kennet and Avon Canal, along which barges used to carry the products of the area to the Thames in the east and to Bristol to the west. The town is built on the steep banks of the River Avon which is crossed by a stone

bridge. Nearly all the houses are of the Bath stone quarried in the area and there are churches of almost every period of English architecture, including a Saxon church. You can also see a great fourteenth-century tithe barn. Nearby are a number of splendid manor houses including Great Chalfield Manor, a moated fifteenth-century house in Gothic-Tudor style, and The Courts, where local weavers would bring their disputes.

Further up the Avon Valley is the pretty village of Lacock. Its Abbey, which became a private mansion after the Reformation, is now cared for by the National Trust. One of its residents was William Henry Fox, pioneer of photography. To the north of Lacock is Chippenham, another stone-built town, which lies just south of the M4 motorway from London to the West Country. On the edge of the Cotswolds is Malmesbury, an old town built on a slope above the Avon, dominated by the ruins of a fine Norman Abbey. From here it is only a short distance to the source of the River Thames, which lies at Thames Head among the Cotswold Hills.

THE GATEWAY
TO
ISLAND BRITAIN

As you travel across the Straits of Dover you are greeted by an impressive and memorable sight; a wall of white cliffs, soaring and dipping along the edge of the sea. These great piles of rock formed by the compressed bones from sea creatures of the Cretaceous Age give the impression of being the outer wall of some different world. From the sea you cannot see behind them; only ambiguous green turf appears above their gleaming sides. Even though we know what lies beyond, a certain sense of mystery persists; perhaps that is why even today passengers on the Channel ferry feel a growing excitement as land is sighted.

The chalky strata wind inland and northward to the London basin, then across to Hampshire, before turning east along the coast to Beachy Head. Here the highest chalk cliff of all plunges seaward, providing the Downs with their most dramatic sight. The great curve of the Downs, lying like a giant horseshoe on its side, embraces a different kind of land where the earth is formed of clay and sedimentary rocks, and where ancient forests have been replaced by woods and fruit orchards. Hedges enclose fields where cattle and sheep graze peacefully by the new motorways that sweep travellers from the Channel ports to London.

The south-east of England, being the nearest part of Britain to the continental mainland, has been the thoroughfare of invaders, as well as more peaceful visitors, ever since Roman times. Julius Caesar, who arrived in AD 55, did no more than pause here before retreating home. It was not until the reign of Claudius that the Roman legions arrived to settle the land. The colonists built roads, villas and towns in this new extension of the Empire, where they believed that gold and silver could be found as well as tin and copper. Having subdued the Britons, whose loose tribal organization was no match for the sophisticated Roman military machine, the Romans began a settlement programme which spread Roman culture throughout Britain. In the south-east they built Stane Street between Canterbury and Chichester and Watling Street from Dover. They built forts along the coast and villas in the inland beauty spots. In the north cities still bear the suffix -caster or -chester, names denoting that they were the site of Roman armed

Rochester, at the mouth of the Medway, was an important naval port along with adjoining Chatham. It has a fine eleventh-century cathedral, castle and several buildings as described in Dickens' Great Expectations *and* Edwin Drood.

camps. As the south-east has no such places, it would seem that the danger of armed revolt by the local inhabitants was remote.

The Romans settled Saxons into this peaceful part of their new conquest. When the Romans withdrew their troops in the fifth century, due to the pressing need for them in Rome, more Saxons arrived, with Angles and Jutes. Unlike the Romans, the new inhabitants preferred a rural life. Soon the Roman cities were neglected and individual farming communities developed in the midst of the countryside. At this time separate kingdoms were set up by rival monarchs throughout Britain.

The arrival of St. Augustine on the Isle of Thanet in 597 brought a new cultural concept into the south-east, then part of the Kingdom of Kent. After the conversion of King Ethelbert to Christianity, a Benedictine monastery was founded at Canterbury. This was followed by a cathedral at Canterbury, and another cathedral at Rochester.

In 1066 the south-east of England was invaded by the Normans, who made England part of the Dukedom of Normandy. Under the Norman kings the barons grew powerful, sometimes forming an uneasy alliance with the bishops of the church, whose long experience in administration (based on Roman models) was an invaluable help in running the country. Castles and abbeys sprang up at Arundel, Chichester, Battle and many other places which were centres of political and economic power.

When the Tudor monarchs established the central power of the monarchy, life in Britain changed once more. Barons relinquished their local power and and became landed gentry, building manor houses like Graveye Manor, Ightam Mote and Scotney, rather than fortresses. Trade with European countries increased the wealth of the south-east and eventually this once embattled corner of England became the peaceful area of countryside inherited by its present population.

Fortunately for the visitor there is little industry in this part of England. Instead there is unspoilt countryside, rich in the architecture, traditions and memories of 2,000 years of English history.

The North Downs

The North Downs stretch across south-east England from the borders of Hampshire to the South Foreland near Dover. At the western end they surge up from Farnham in a great rounded mound appropriately called the Hog's Back. From here there are views to the north over the Aldershot Plain, home of the British Army, and Farnborough, headquarters of the Royal Air Force Establishment and site of the annual International Air Show. To the south is downland, some of it inaccessible when the Army is on manoeuvres. Also to the south are the Frensham Ponds, now a popular place for picnickers, fishermen and amateur sailors. Once, it seems, this area had more sinister visitors; at Frensham church there is a witches' cauldron and, not far away, there are three hills known as the Devil's Jumps.

The great cathedral of Canterbury lies in the old town which is surrounded by city walls and the River Stour. The cathedral is near the original abbey founded by St. Augustine in 598.

Top: Guildford High Street slopes steeply down to the River Wey and has many picturesque buildings including the seventeenth-century Town Hall.

At the eastern end of the Hog's Back lies Guildford, a Dickensian kind of town. In its steep High Street you will find a fine coaching inn, the Angel Hotel, and in Quarry Street there is the keep of a castle built by Henry II. In contrast to Guildford's Tudor and Georgian centre is modern Guildford, symbolized by the red brick cathedral and the University of Surrey.

Beyond Guildford lies Dorking. Here the Roman Stane Street crossed the Pilgrims Way, which ran along the North Downs to Canterbury. Some of the Downs' highest hills are around Dorking. Box Hill lies to the north and Leith Hill (294 m;

965 ft) to the south. There are also some splendid manor houses in the vicinity – Loseley House, Clandon Park, Hatchlands and Polesden Lacey, a Georgian villa remodelled at the turn of the century.

Around Redhill and Reigate the southern borders of Greater London run perilously close to the North Downs and the northern slopes have begun to look like an extension of suburbia. This part of Kent lies on the lower slopes of the North Downs where the Weald begins and since there is no precise boundary could be said to be in either area.

As the North Downs approach Maidstone their northern flank overlooks the Medway and Thames Estuary. At one time the nation's shipyards were hard at work there, producing the ships that enabled Britain to become mistress of the seas. Today Chatham and Rochester, though still busy towns, have lost their seafaring connections. Maidstone lies on the bnks of the River

Left: Fourteenth-century All Saints church and the Bishops Palace lie by the River Medway in Maidstone, an important county town in Kent.

Below: Polesden Lacey, near Great Bookham, was built in 1824 in a beautiful 900-acre park. The home is elegantly furnished and contains a fine collection of paintings.

Medway, which used to be very busy with barges carrying Kentish timber and iron to the shipyards at its mouth, past the building that was once an Archbishops' palace. The countryside around Maidstone is delightful, with small villages where you can see medieval cottages. There is Lenham, near to moated Leeds Castle, and Aylesford, on the Medway River, which has an active Carmelite friary where visitors are welcome.

On the eastern slope of the Downs, as they turn south across the tip of Kent, is Canterbury. The towers of the cathedral rise above the city, which has preserved its medieval walls and one of its seven formidable entrance gates. From the hills around Canterbury the Rivers Stour and Lit wend their way to the flat, sandy coast of east Kent. On their banks there are many delightful villages like Fordwich, Patrixbourne and Wickhambreux – well worth a detour for anyone visiting the cathedral city.

The North Downs come to an abrupt end at Dover, providing a glorious view of the English Channel from grassy hilltops which extend eastward to North Foreland and south-west to Folkestone on the very edge of the Downs.

The South Downs

The South Downs are shorter and narrower than the North Downs. They are also less wooded. The south-west winds sweeping up the Channel inhibit the growth of vegetation except at the eastern end, where there is a wide coastal plain. The downland country north of Chichester is charming – there are little villages like the Hartings and the Marsdens, between which lies Uppark, a Queen Anne house in which Nelson's mistress Emma once lived. To the east of Uppark is Goodwood, the famous

Lord Culpepper, Governor of Virginia, had his home in Leeds Castle between 1680 and 1683. Part of the castle dates back to the thirteenth century and its moat and isolated position give it a fairy-tale air.

The Earl Marshall of England, the Duke of Norfolk, owns Arundel Castle on the slopes of the Downs above the River Arun. The castle was badly damaged by Cromwell's troops but was restored in a thirteenth-century style.

racecourse, and Goodwood House which was owned by the Duke of Richmond.

Few rivers cut across the smooth slopes of the Downs but, at Arundel, the River Arun has eroded a passage to the sea, guarded by the formidable Arundel Castle. The Castle, set in extensive grounds, overlooks the attractive town below and the coastal plain which invaders had to cross. Arundel Castle is the home of the Duke of Norfolk, Earl Marshall of England, but is open to the public in the summer. At that time of year the Norfolk Arms, a coaching inn, is crowded with motorists touring the sights around Arundel which include a Roman villa at Bignor and an Elizabethan house at Parham, about three miles to the north.

Still further north, in the depths of rural downland, are Petersfield and Midhurst. You will also find Petworth, where Turner spent some time. Here he painted some of his colourful avant-garde abstracts as well as more conventional views, and some of his paintings can be seen in the gallery at Petworth House.

The Downs approach the coast at Worthing, creating the landscape of white cliffs and rounded grassy hills that is the quintessence of the south-east. An ancient hilltrack runs parallel to the sea, along which are burial mounds; and you can see the circular ramparts of Iron Age settlements like Cissbury Ring and Chanctonbury Ring, the latter easily identified by the clump of beech trees planted in it by the owner of Wiston Park, an Elizabethan house nearby.

The heights of the South Downs command magnificent views across the Weald to the North Downs and southward across the English Channel. Since Elizabethan times they have provided an excellent site for the beacons which were lit to warn other ports, and the government in London, of the approach of enemy ships. Ditchling Beacon was one such place, and another was Firle Beacon on the east side of the Ouse valley.

Lewes is situated on the slopes of the valley of the River Ouse and, because of its strategic position, has been an important town since Norman times. It still preserves a Norman castle among its narrow side streets where medieval houses still exist, dating back to 1264 when Simon de Montfort's troops passed through Lewes and defeated Henry III. The village of Glynde and Glynde House, a sixteenth-century mansion, are to the east of Lewes, as is Glyndebourne Opera House, a centre for the great British social and operatic summer season.

The final eastern surge of the South Downs rises to more than 213 m (700 ft) above the green valley of the River Cuckmere, where there is a fine priory at Michelham and Charleston House, south of Lullington. In the heights, above the village of Wilmington, you can see the mysterious figure of a man cut into the chalk which, according to one legend, is Harold, the last Saxon King of England, who was defeated at Hastings in 1066.

The Weald

Between the North and South Downs lies green countryside with the remains of forests that once covered the whole of Kent. In the centre of this area is the Weald which, due to the rich sedimentary soil, is one of the most fertile regions in Britain. Once the forests had been cleared, farmers began to exploit the land. Small farms were set up around the castles of powerful barons, who offered protection in return for military service and taxes. Numerous little centres of life developed in this way, focused around either a castle or an abbey, and the buildings which remain today add to the interests of the Kentish countryside. Several of these centres lay between Sevenoaks and Royal Tunbridge Wells, in the green valleys watered by the River Medway and its tributaries – the Eden and the Beult.

Sevenoaks is surrounded by villages and woods which today provide rewarding destinations for motorists and walkers. To the west lies Westerham, and the home of General Wolfe; nearby at Chartwell is the house of Winston Churchill, much as it was when he lived there. To the south is one of the most evocative of moated

Top right: There are some fine views from the Downs above Wilmington which lies in typical Sussex countryside on the road to Eastbourne.

Right: Wakehurst Place in Sussex has beautiful gardens administered by the Royal Botanical Gardens of Kew.

manor houses, Ightham Mote, hidden in a wooded valley. And at Old Soar you can see a rare example of the stone house of a medieval knight, comfortable but by no means luxurious.

In Sevenoaks is Knole Park, home of the Sackville-West family. The house was enlarged by one of their ancestors in Tudor times. A more recent descendant was Vita Sackville-West, creator, with her husband Harold Nicolson, of that beautiful garden at Sissinghurst.

South of Sevenoaks is Tonbridge. Once the busy embarcation point for Weald timber which was sent down the Medway to the Rochester shipyards, it is now a tranquil place where cruisers ply the river and fishermen line its banks. West of Tonbridge the Medway is joined by the River Eden and along its valley you will find the splendid house and grounds of Penshurst Place, the home of Sir Philip Sydney's family for 400 years, with a fine collection of paintings in its picture gallery. Also along the Eden is Chiddingstone, where the oast houses with their conical roofs are grouped together like a conclave of monks and a little further west Hever Castle, home of the Boleyn family.

Royal Tunbridge Wells, to the south, was once one of Britain's most fashionable spas. Here elegant ladies and gentlemen strolled under the colonnades of the Pantiles, took the waters and gossiped, as did their friends who went to Bath or Harrogate. You can still walk along the terraces where Henrietta Maria, wife of Charles I, sat with her friends, but you will not be able to take the waters whose source can be seen along the promenade.

Leaving Royal Tunbridge Wells and heading towards the coast, as the Weald descends into the flat marshlands by the sea, you will find some lovely places to visit. There is one of the most delightful and domesticated castles in England, Scotney. This is an example of the way fourteenth-century castles were adapted to the more civilized life that evolved with the stable monarchy of the 1600s. The moat became a decorative pond and the land around it a garden with a most romantic atmosphere. To the south-east there

Faversham Creek empties at low tide leaving barges and sailing boats high and dry by derelict warehouses that once stored merchandise or were engaged in the oyster trade.

are many villages and manor houses. Hawkhurst is the centre of this area which includes Sissinghurst Castle, Great Dixter manor house at Northiam, and the ruins of Bothiam. South of Scotney you can visit Rudyard Kipling's house in Burwash, where an old water mill still grinds corn into flour.

The Coast

The coast of south-east England is surprisingly varied. In north Kent there are the tidal mudbanks of the Thames Estuary, once full of tiny villages that depended on the sea for their existence but now the victims of silting. As the estuary opens up into the North Sea the landscape changes. Beaches which played a historic part in the development of the concept of workers' leisure come into view along the coast.

Margate was the most popular destination for the wherrys and, later, the paddle steamers that introduced thousands of working-class Londoners to the delights of the seaside. Ramsgate and Broadstairs, round the point of North Foreland, were patronized by a slightly better class of person – or at least they thought themselves to be! Dickens, who lived at Broadstairs, thought otherwise and constantly complained that the noise of trippers, brass bands and street entertainers prevented him from working. However he did complete David Copperfield there.

The east coast from Broadstairs to Dover has a different character – the low cliffs giving way to flat marshes and sand dunes. Although Sandwich, which was once on the sea, is now far inland, Deal and nearby Walmer (one of the Cinque ports committed to provide ships and money for the defence of Henry VIII's England) have managed to hang on to their seashore location. This historic coast which has seen so many invasions is a peaceful place today, where the only danger to the walker or bird-watcher might be a flying golf ball from one of the many courses that have been established on this extensive coastal plain.

Top: Whitstable oysters were enjoyed many years ago by the Romans and they are still cultivated in this North Kent seaside town facing the Isle of Sheppey.

'Any invaders attempting to land at Dover would soon have been deterred by the forbiddingly sheer cliffs which continue all the way to Folkestone. Dover and Folkestone are the main ports for Channel crossings and Dover is the proposed terminal for the Channel tunnel.

The coast beyond Hythe positively invites illegal entry and has long been the favourite landing place for smugglers and, more recently, illegal immigrants. Two great marshy areas make up this part of the south-east coast. One is Romney Marsh and the other Walland Marsh, which stretches out to Dungeness Point and provides a home for an airport at Lydd and a nuclear power station at Denge Marsh. The largest town on the Marshes is New Romsey, a popular place with train enthusiasts, who crowd on to the miniature railway that runs across the marsh to Hythe.

From the Marshes to Chichester the south coast resorts dominate the shoreline, most of them the products of speculation during the railway age. Rich entrepreneurs encouraged the new holiday business by intense promotion of the health-giving properties of sea water, advising that it should be imbibed with milk or brandy (according to taste), and later bathed in – at first in the privacy of a bath and later in public.

Hastings was a fishing village at the time of the great seaside holiday promotion but was soon developing the visitors' residential area which, even today, distinguishes the west side of the town from the east. Bexhill and Eastbourne were specially developed to offer the 'better' classes of society a seaside resort without the vulgarity of those visited by the working classes.

Brighton was once a little fishing village called Brighthelmstone. The original village was in the area now known as The Lanes. Brighton was the most successful of the south coast villages turned resort, and was given an extra fillip by the support of George IV. He persuaded Nash, the architect of the elegant

Left: Charles Dickens lived and wrote parts of Barnaby Rudge *and* David Copperfield *at Bleak House, which overlooks the busy harbour at Broadstairs.*

Below: Dover Castle stands in a commanding position above the white cliffs that lie behind busy Dover harbour, the most important port for cross-Channel traffic. In the castle is the Roman Pharos, or lighthouse.

Regents Park terraces, to produce the delightful extravaganza of the Royal Pavilion. Since its beginnings as a gathering place for the more rakish members of London society, Brighton has never looked back. In summer it is crowded with visitors enjoying the endless carnival of its streets and promenades. In winter it is a popular location for conferences and other serious activities of the business world.

Whatever drawbacks Brighton may have for the visitor who dislikes crowds, there is no doubt that it is the archetypal south-coast resort. All the ingredients are there: the Georgian architecture and the piers; the promenades with their wrought-iron lamps and the modern leisure centre; the rehabilitated grand hotels and the bow-fronted seaside boarding houses; plus a variety of shops from smart little boutiques to stalls selling false teeth made of sugar candy. Almost anything goes at Brighton, but Hove, next

The Seven Sisters cliffs run along the Sussex coast where the Cuckmere River breaks through the South Downs at Birling Gap.

The broad shingle beach at Brighton runs from the Marina to the pier and beyond to Hove. Along the cliffs, elegant houses date from the period when the Prince Regent built the exotic Pavilion.

door, and Worthing, Littlehampton and Bognor Regis all present a more respectable face, and are popular locations for traditional family holidays.

Chichester, the most westerly of the resorts, provides a complete contrast. Chichester has far too long a history to have changed its character for the benefit of its visitors. The town existed even before the arrival of the Romans, who made the king of the Chichester area their viceroy. In the centre of the town is the square where the lovely eleventh-century cathedral stands, with little streets of shops, boutiques and restaurants around it. Much of the architecture is Georgian. This is especially evident in the streets named East, West, North and South Palant.

Around Chichester are flat marshy areas, their rivers and canals crowded with boats and nearby is Fishbourne, where a Roman villa with fine mosaic floors was discovered in 1960. The villa was built in about AD 70 and perhaps marks the success of the Roman occupation of south-east England in a port where the Claudian invaders of AD 43 had kept their stores during their first attempts at colonization.

THE FARMLANDS
OF
CONSTABLE
COUNTRY

Nowhere in Britain is there such an extensive region of wide open spaces as along the east coast from south of the Humber to the Thames Estuary. As Constable's paintings bear witness, this is a landscape of gently undulating hills, flat river valleys, and small villages – all under a magnificent sky, often clearer here than in other parts of the country.

In East Anglia a ridge of low hills, a continuation of the Chilterns, curves diagonally across Essex, Suffolk and Norfolk, making a watershed between the coastal plain, the flat marshland of the fens and the agricultural plains of Cambridgeshire. In the north the flat fenland stretches toward Lincolnshire, where the unrelieved plain is broken by two low ridges of hills. One is the Lincoln Edge, separating the valleys of the River Trent and the River Witham, and the other the Lincolnshire Wolds, between the River Witham and the sea.

In the Dark Ages, when Europe was invaded by fierce tribes from beyond the eastern boundaries of the Roman Empire, the east of England was vulnerable to attack. Usually the Norsemen who sailed across the North Sea in their longships, and the Angles and Saxons of Northern Europe, came to pillage and destroy. Some, however, settled, building villages and castles on the higher parts of the swampy land. Later, in the days when Christianity was being established, great churches were built, some of them like protective fortresses around which the life of the community developed.

In the seventeenth century much of the swampy land was reclaimed, thanks to the expertise of the Dutch who brought with them experience gained from draining and defending their own low-lying country by the sea. The Dutch set up a system of drainage and ditches, planted new crops and introduced their style of architecture in villages and towns, thus giving a distinctive look to the houses of East Anglia. They also set up trading undertakings which led to the development of ports like Harwich and Ipswich. Today the east of England continues with its traditional activities and its links with The Netherlands and Scandinavia are still strong. In addition, the east coast, with its superb sands and long cloudless

The pretty Essex village of Finchingfield has a Norman church, named after St. John the Baptist, and picturesque cottages surrounding the village green and its duck pond.

The Great Ouse wends its way in a leisurely fashion through the Fens past Stretham, south of Ely. Stretham, seen on the horizon, is a village with sixteenth- and eighteenth-century houses.

days, has become an important summer holiday region with large popular resorts like Clacton-on-Sea, Southend-on-Sea and Great Yarmouth, and smaller, more secluded villages like Aldeburgh, Southwold and Blakeney on the north coast of Norfolk.

The Coastal Plain

Numerous small rivers flow from the East Anglian hills into the estuaries that are a feature of the Essex and Suffolk coasts, providing safe sailing and sheltered bathing for visitors. Nearest to London, on the estuary of the Thames, is Southend which started life as a competitor to the resorts of north Kent. Owing to the silting up of the shore, it had to extend is pier until it became the longest in Britain. Nowadays Southend is a large town in its own right with a civic and commercial centre. Its seafront, however, still provides all the fun of the fair. Further up the coast, past the yachting havens of Burnham-on-Crouch and Maldon, is another large popular resort. Clacton-on-Sea, a handsome Victorian town, lies up the Blackwater Estuary where, among other vessels, there are numerous well-restored Thames sailing barges which take part in barge races during the summer. Another feature of Clacton is its broad pier, which contains a swimming pool, a fairground and various other entertainments. A long promenade runs behind the pier.

Along the coast to the east you can see several of the Martello towers which were built all round the south-east coast in the early nineteenth century to repel a possible invasion by Napoleon. Inland lies the Priory of St. Osyth, founded by the wife of an East Anglican king of the seventh century who was martyred by the Danes. The present priory, which is the largest monastic complex in England, was built on the ruins of the original convent and some of the buildings date back to the thirteenth century.

If you follow the River Colne inland you will arrive in Colchester, the first major Roman town in England, built by Claudius in AD 50. Relics of the Roman occupation can be seen at the Balkerne Gate and in the Colchester and Essex Museum. There are also Roman remains in the vaults of the Norman castle. The castle is the largest of its type in England and was built over a Claudian temple. A reminder of the part the later Romans played in establishing Christianity throughout Europe is the statue of St. Helena, mother of the Emperor Constantine, who rescued many of the Christian relics from Jerusalem and founded numerous churches.

North of Colchester, on the estuaries of the rivers Stour and Orwell, is Harwich – a port from which the ferry to the Hook of Holland runs. Most of the great Elizabethan sailors kept their ships at Harwich, including Drake, Frobisher and Raleigh. In later days,

Burnham-on-Crouch is a popular yachting centre with an elegant High Street with Georgian houses and a picturesque and bustling quayside.

Top: Artist John Constable's family owned Flatford Mill, inspiration for several of his masterpieces. Today, it is a centre for field study.

Above: Woodbridge, on the River Deben, has a well-maintained old tidal mill, now a museum, and a quayside lively with the activities of boatyards.

Nelson's ships were moored here. Samuel Pepys, who was Secretary of the Admiralty, lived here and the *Mayflower*, with the Pilgrim Fathers aboard, set off from Harwich on the way to Plymouth and from there to the New World.

The estuary of the Stour leads inland to Constable country. The most famous painter of the English landscape was born at East Bergholt in 1776 amid the green fields and watermills that so often appear in his paintings. His family owned several mills; one of them at Flatford, where Willy Lott's cottage still stands, looking

Once a busy port of the River Orwell, Ipswich has many features of historical interest, including the Ancient House and Christchurch Mansion, now a museum.

much as it does in the painting of the *Hay Wain*. Even after he became well-known and moved to London, Constable kept returning to the Stour. Here he did many of his famous paintings such as *Dedham Vale, Flatford Mill* and *The Leaping Horse*. Constable's parents and Willy Lott are buried in the churchyard at East Bergholt; Constable himself lies in Hampstead, London. Further up the Stour is Sudbury, the birthplace of another great painter, Gainsborough who was born in Sudbury in 1727 and who was to become one of the most fashionable portrait painters of his age. However, his real inclination was for landscape and especially the landscapes of his youth. The Tudor house in which he lived as a boy is now a museum.

The other great estuary by Harwich is the Orwell which leads inland to Ipswich, the county town of Suffolk. The town became important as a result of the wool trade and continues to be a port although, at one time, silting of the estuary threatened to close the docks. Ipswich is the birthplace of Cardinal Wolsey, Chancellor of England and builder of Hampton Court, and there are a number of Tudor houses in the town.

Between Harwich and Lowestoft the coast is low-lying and almost uninhabited, owing to the danger of flooding. However, you will find the exceptionally attractive village of Aldeburgh along this shore. It has a picturesque front of old cottages, some converted into pubs, and a Moot Hall dating back to the sixteenth century. Aldeburgh is famous as the home of a music festival at which many premiers have been given. One of these was *Peter Grimes* by Benjamin Britten: based on a poem by George Crabbe, the opera recounts the story of the area in the eighteenth century. Performances take place at The Maltings concert hall, the design of which is based on the character of the malt store that once stood on the site of the present building.

The coast in this area is prone to erosion by the sea which, as in the case of Dunwich to the north, has sometimes demolished whole towns. All that remains of Dunwich are fragments of the old priory among the sand dunes and marran grass, now inhabited by large numbers of sea birds and waders. Two memorable little towns along this coast are Walberswick and Southwold which flank the River Hythe and retain the character of Edwardian villages. Southwold has ivy-covered, timbered and brick buildings. The set of guns you can see on the grassy slopes of Gun Hill was a present from George II and replaced a set given to the town by Charles I to protect the inhabitants from the Dunkirk pirates.

North of Southwold lies Lowestoft, famous for its kippers. It was here that the fishermen who fished the Dogger Bank and other North Sea fishing grounds kept their boats in the great days of herring fishing. Those days are now over, due to overfishing, but trawlers still bring in cod, plaice and the other fast-diminishing fish of the once abundant sea. Deprived of much of its fishing livelihood, Lowestoft has now developed other small industries and has also become a popular summer holiday resort as it has a good beach to the south of the port.

Further north is the large resort of Great Yarmouth, which manages to live a double life with great success. Along its four-mile seafront there are promenades, fun fairs, amusement parks and everything that the holiday visitor could want in the way of food and entertainment. However, behind the housing, along the banks of the Yar, the town has a completely different side to its character. Here, running parallel to the sea to the south of Great Yarmouth, you will find docks and quaysides. There are narrow streets called The Rows – one of them less than 1 m (3 ft) wide – and a thirteenth-century Toll House with dungeons in its basement. On the South Quay there is an Elizabethan Museum housed in a building erected in 1596.

Great Yarmouth is the entry point to the Norfolk Broads, a wonderland of lakes and rivers, providing a superb boating and yachting area, good fishing and peaceful, traffic-free countryside for summer leisure seekers. There are 30 broads altogether, inter-connected by rivers and canals. Along their banks you will find little villages, waterside pubs and workshops where old crafts like thatching are still carried on. Here and there windmills turn in the breezes that keep the skies clear of clouds.

The superb Norman cathedral with its soaring spire dominates the city of Norwich on the River Wensum. Near the cathedral is the formidable castle built by the Norman Henry I to pacify the rebellious East Anglians.

On the western side of The Broads, in a bend on the River
Wensum, is the cathedral city of Norwich. Norwich is over 1,000
years old and appears on coins minted for Athelstan. Some believe
that it may even have been Boadicea's capital. In the centre of the
city stands the massive Norman castle built by Henry I which has
an unusual blind arcade decoration. Rarely seen in Norman architecture in England, this decoration is common on the Norman
buildings erected in Sicily. The castle houses a museum where the
work of the Norwich School of painters can be seen. The Norwich
School, of which John Crome and John Sell Cotman were the two
chief exponents, was a group of eighteenth-century painters of
Norfolk scenery following in the footsteps of Gainsborough and
the Dutch painters such as Meindert Hobbema and Aelbert Cuyp.
By the castle is the extensive market place with its many colourful
stalls. It stands in a square surrounded by fine buildings from
several architectural periods and two churches – the Church of St.
Peter Mancroft and Norwich Parish Church.

To the north-east of the castle rises the splendid cathedral,
with a fine Norman tower capped by a spire added in the fifteenth
century. Construction of the cathedral was begun by Bishop
Losinga in the twelfth century and the building has retained its
original design. The interior has a magnificent 124 m (407 ft) nave
with massive Norman columns. The vaulted roof has bosses
depicting stories from the Old and New Testaments. The choir has
an ambulatory and radiating chapels in the continental style.
Behind is the eighth-century Bishop's Throne. There is a fine
two-storey cloister to the south of the cathedral and between the
church and river there is a considerable amount of open ground on
which stand the Bishops Palace and the Great Hospital. Norwich is

Sandringham, the royal home in Norfolk, though Jacobean in appearance, was built in 1870 by Edward VII, when he was Prince of Wales. The house and grounds are open to the public except when the Royal Family are in residence.

particularly rich in churches; there are five in St. Benedict Street alone. Many of these churches were built before the Reformation by wealthy merchants involved in the weaving and dying industries for which Norwich was famous.

The flat, fertile countryside to the north of Norwich and The Broads has a mysterious and sometimes misty coast where the land has encroached on the sea. Salt marshes have left former seaside villages inland; high but not completely dry, they can only be reached from the sea by canals cut through the green turfy marshland. The names of the villages – Cley next the sea, Wells-next-to-the-sea and Holne-next-to-the-sea – tell their own tale. Despite the loss of a seashore, many villages along this coast continue to glean a living from the sea. Villagers harvest whelks, clams, mussels, crabs and other crustacea, and also fish for the cod, plaice and eels found in this area. From Cromer – a pleasant old resort with a famous lifeboat station – to Hunstanton, the coast runs from east to west, ending in a layer of multi-coloured cliffs overlooking The Wash.

In the hinterland there are many fine estates including 7,000-acre Sandringham, owned by the Royal Family. There is also Holkham Hall, the manor house of Thomas Coke whose innovations in agriculture changed the face of farming. The Hall has a fine art gallery with English and Italian paintings. Castle Rising, near Kings Lynn, is a Norman building by William de Albini.

Kings Lynn, though much rebuilt, still possesses some of the old buildings from the days when it was a great eighteenth-century port. Among these are the Customs House, and the Guildhall founded in the fifteenth century.

Around the Fens

The Wash, the sandy beach between Norfolk and Lincolnshire, is best remembered as the place where King John managed to lose all the royal jewels in a quicksand. In those days The Wash extended much further inland. The flat, featureless land extends westwards; first through the swampy ground of The Fens, then on through reclaimed land where market gardens and farms profit from the rich alluvial soil that stretches into Cambridgeshire. The rivers that water this land flow from the centre of England; the Welland from near Market Harborough in Leicestershire, the Nene from near Arbury Hill in Northamptonshire, and the Great Ouse from near Buckingham. The tributaries of the Great Ouse, however, come from the western slopes of the low hills of East Anglia.

At the southern end of these hills is Saffron Walden, on the watershed between the River Cam which flows north to join the Great Ouse, and the River Chelmer flowing south through Chelmsford. Saffron Walden is an old town with many medieval houses built with money from the wool trade and, as its name suggests, the saffron industry. On the western outskirts of the town is Audley Park, one of the finest Jacobean mansions in England. The house was built by Thomas Howard, Earl of Suffolk, and contains some elegant interiors by Robert Adam. To the south of Saffron Walden is another great house, Stansted Mountfichet, which is in the territory in dispute over the building of a third London airport. Also within jet noise of the airport would be The Rodings, a delightful and secluded group of eight villages situated along the River Roding. Nearby is Great Dunmow. Once every four years this is the scene of an unusual ceremony when married couples who have not quarrelled over the past year are presented with a flitch of bacon.

Further north along the Suffolk hills is Bury St. Edmunds on the River Lark. Bury became a resting place for the body of the

Saffron Walden has much interesting architecture, including the Sun Inn which is decorated with plasterwork from the time of Charles II.

During the fifteenth-century, when Lavenham was an important centre of the wool trade, it acquired many fine buildings, including the timbered Guild Hall.

martyred St. Edmund in the ninth century and, in the eleventh century, King Canute made the monastery built by St. Edmund into an abbey. The abbey is now a ruin, though pieces of it can still be seen in the public gardens. There is, however, a magnificent Norman tower nearby and, next to it, the church of St. James where Mary Tudor is buried.

Thetford is situated on the Little Ouse in a region of heathland on the borders of Norfolk and Suffolk known as Breckland. There are many traces of prehistoric man around here, including burial chambers, a flint mine at Grimes Graves and many barrows scattered about the open country. However, the best find for archaeologists in the area was the Roman treasure of Mildenhall, on the Icknield Way, which is now in the British Museum. On the western edge of the fens stand some of the most important towns in East Anglia. To the south-east is Cambridge. The loveliest of university cities, it is built along the River Cam which flows peacefully past the green lawns behind the colleges.

Cambridge University was established in the thirteenth century as a centre of learning. Teachers gathered there and were joined by students who did not, at that time, have special colleges to reside in. As in Oxford, the early centuries of university life were turbulent; students were usually at war with the townspeople and had less respect for law and order than they had for learning! The first college was Peterhouse, established by the Bishop of Ely. It stands at the eastern end of the Cam, near to the Fitzwilliam Museum which has an extensive collection of antiquities and paintings by the great masters as well as more modern works.

Following the river west, along the lawns known as The Backs, you pass Queens' College and then King's. King's College chapel is one of the finest examples of the Perpendicular style of Gothic architecture in the world; begun by Henry VI but not completed until 1515, after the Wars of the Roses. Among the chapel's great glories are its fan tracery roof, Rubens' *Adoration of the Magi* and – less tangible perhaps but no less sublime – the Kings College choir.

After Kings came Trinity, founded by Henry VIII in 1546 and attended by such famous men as Newton, Bacon, Byron and Macaulay. Beyond is St. Johns, with its famous Bridge of Sighs (actually New Bridge) across the Cam. Other colleges can be seen on Kings Parade, Sydney Street and Jesus Lane, all located in the town. Cambridge is a busy place, especially when there is a market in front of fifteenth-century St. Mary's church. Around St. Mary's

Below: The River Cam flows peacefully past numerous colleges of Cambridge University, including Queens', and provides quiet waters for romantic punt trips.

are some of the most important buildings in the town centre, among them the Guildhall, Bacon's tobacco shop and the Senate House, built by James Gibbs in the eighteenth century.

The countryside near Cambridge is largely flat. However, a slight eminence known as the Gog and the Magog Hills provide some views over the area; in particular of the towers and spires of Cambridge. Across to the west you may see the village of Grant-chester, about which the poet Rupert Brooke wrote with longing during the First World War:

'Stands the Church clock at ten to three?
And is there honey still for tea?'

To the north-west of Cambridge, across flat farmlands on the Great Ouse river, is Huntingdon. This small town was the birthplace of Oliver Cromwell in 1599. The house that first heard the voice of the Lord Protector is now the Huntingdon Research Centre and the school he attended has been made into a museum of his life. Hitchingbrooke House, the Cromwell's family home, is on the outskirts of the town.

Near Huntingdon there are several attractive little villages situated along the banks of the Great Ouse. St. Ives has a picturesque fifteenth-century stone bridge, with a chapel on its centre, and in the streets you can see many half-timbered houses; Hemmingford Grey and its sister village Hemmingford Abbots, where the river winds through grassy banks overhung with trees, have thatched cottages and half-timbered buildings, evoking images of eighteenth-century rural England. Buckden village is nearby, with its splendid Bishops Palace. Built for the Bishops of Lincoln, it was used by Henry VIII as a haven for his divorced wife Katharine of Aragon. Katharine was later moved to Kimbolton Castle where she spent the last four years of her life. You can take a boat from St. Ives to St. Neots or vice versa, and this section of the Great Ouse is well worth exploring by water.

To the north of Huntingdon lies Little Gidding, the setting of one of T. S. Eliot's finest later poems *Little Gidding*. To the east is Ely, isolated in the Fens, once an island from which Hereward the Wake defied the Normans. Later, the land was reclaimed from the water and became part of the farmlands which have stretched across the countryside since the eighteenth century.

There is an unusual cathedral at Ely which stands out like a lighthouse in the flat landscape. It was built by Simeon, twelfth-century Abbot of Ely, and rebuilt in the thirteenth century to provide a shrine for St. Ethelred, founder of the first abbey on the site in the seventh century. The cathedral still contains much of the original Norman architecture, but its imposing central tower was built in the fourteenth century, after the original tower collapsed.

Another great cathedral in the western part of the Fens is Peterborough. Though now deprived of the old town which once clustered round the Close, the cathedral retains all its former glory. An earlier church on the site was sacked by Hereward the Wake, which may explain why the present cathedral, built by the Normans, has a solid fortress-like look. The west front, added in the 1300s, is magnificent and leads into a spacious nave. There are two transepts, in one of which you can see the tombs of bishops of

Left: Hinxworth, on the Hertfordshire/Bedfordshire border has retained its rural character and has thatched cottages, a medieval church and pub.

the original Saxon church. In the chancel is Katharine of Aragon's grave and a stone slab marking the place where Mary Queen of Scots was buried before her son, James I, removed the body to Westminster Abbey in 1612.

Lincolnshire

The Lincoln Ridge, running up the centre of Lincolnshire, begins at the ancient town of Stamford on the Cambridgeshire border. Stamford, because of its position on rising land, has been a Roman camp, a Danish headquarters and the site of a Norman castle (of which only a few stones remain today). In medieval times Stamford was an important wool town and its many lovely stone buildings date back to this period. The River Welland winds its way slowly through the town below the church of St. Mary, whose elegant thirteenth-century spire can be seen for miles around. Five other medieval churches are scattered through the town. Stamford was given to William Cecil by Elizabeth I for his wise counsel to her court. He became Lord Burghley and built a handsome mansion a mile to the south of the town.

Lincolnshire is a relatively lightly-inhabited county and its towns and villages are widely separated. On the road to Lincoln from Stamford is the town of Grantham, once a busy crossroads until the railway and the M1 motorway were built. Situated on the River Witham, Grantham is a very old town and contains the thirteenth-century church of St. Wulfram, with the Saint's grave in its crypt. There are several medieval buildings around the church and The Angel and Royal Hotel has a fifteenth-century gate. A previous inn on the site of the hotel was used as a court by King John. On the way to Lincoln from Grantham you pass Stragglethorpe Hall where the most northern vineyard in Europe produces white wine from the grapes grown on the slopes of Lincoln Edge.

Lincoln is really two towns: the new industrial town by the River Witham and the old town on the limestone ridge, dominated by the superb cathedral, once a Roman stronghold. Not a great deal remains of the Roman town from which eastern England was ruled, except the massive Newport Arch to the north of the cathedral, the foundations of the East Gate and stones marking the position of columns on an important building in Ballgate.

When the Normans arrived they built a castle, using some of the Roman masonry. The entrance to the castle is through a massive fourteenth-century gate on Castle Hill, off Ballgate. The Normans appointed Bishop Remigius to Lincoln, with instructions to build another church on the site of a former church which had been administered from the Abbey of Dorchester on Thames. Unlike many cathedrals which have taken centuries to build, Lincoln was originally erected in 20 years. This may account for its powerful unity of form. The west front is particularly compelling with its tall central portal and colonnaded façade, reminiscent of northern Italian architecture. Three great towers topped with pinnacles complete the imposing aspect of the third largest cathedral in Britain.

The cathedral is enhanced by the old village which still surrounds it. Well-maintained buildings which have been converted into shops selling antiques, books, prints and other goods are set along narrow streets, evoking the life of the town before the industrial age.

From the tower of the cathedral you can look east to the North Sea across the Lincolnshire Wolds. Sheep graze on the gentle hillsides and market gardeners in the valleys busily prepare produce for the Grimsby frozen food factories. Beyond this

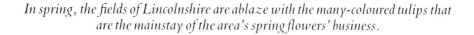

In spring, the fields of Lincolnshire are ablaze with the many-coloured tulips that are the mainstay of the area's spring flowers' business.

The destruction of the Norman cathedral by an earthquake in 1185 gave Bishop Hugh of Avalon the opportunity to erect the magnificent building that today dominates the skyline from a ridge above the city of Lincoln.

sparsely populated region lies the sea. There is the summer resort of Cleethorpes, near the fishing and industrial port of Grimsby, Mablethorpe, a popular holiday area with many caravan and bungalow sites and Skegness, queen of the Lincolnshire coast, with extensive sands and plenty of entertainment. Few people live

permanently along this coast as its low-lying shore is liable to flooding. However, its sand dunes and lonely marshlands are ideal for nature reserves, of which there are several, including one at Theddlethorpe St. Helens and another south of Skegness.

The southern area of the Lincolnshire coast has been utilized for the cultivation of bulb plants – once more with the help of the Dutch, who started up the tulip industry some 60 years ago. Today the growing of spring bulbs provides employment to thousands of people in Boston and Spalding and attracts thousands more in April and May to see the colourful acres of tulips, daffodils and other spring flowers.

GREEN COUNTRYSIDE
—AND—
MANOR HOUSES

On its journey through southern England, the Thames flows through eight counties; and, with its tributaries, draws water from the Cotswolds, the Chiltern Hills and the Berkshire Downs. Since Roman times the wide spread of the Thames river system has provided the vital connections between London and the Midlands so necessary for military and commercial operations. During the industrial age, the valleys of the Thames system became carriers of canals, and corridors through which railway lines reached western and central England. Today, railways and canals have been replaced by motorways which, on the whole, have skirted the Thames Valley and tributaries. Only along its low course, as it approaches London, is the tranquility of the great river shattered by the sound of juggernauts. The area surrounding the Thames river system has remained remarkably unspoilt since the days when it was first used as a waterway. The villages, and the countryside around them, are truly rural – even though today many of the ancient brick and flint cottages are inhabited by people who work in London or one of the other urban centres along the course of the Thames.

Because of the wide area that this great river system covers its landscape is extremely varied. In the Cotswolds, where the Thames is born, there are gentle hills sloping up to the western ridge where they suddenly drop into the valley of the Severn. In the Berkshire Downs the rounded chalk hills predominate. From their bare tops you can enjoy lovely views of rolling countryside, sometimes covered in wheat fields, and sometimes green with grass, where thoroughbred racehorses exercise under the watchful eye of their trainers. In the Chilterns, the landscape changes again. The hills are covered in beech trees, providing the timber for the traditional furniture-making trade that has been carried out around High Wycombe since the Middle Ages.

In many ways the Thames is a secretive river. If you travel along it by boat, or on foot along the tow path, you will be rewarded by glimpses of great houses and gardens not visible from the road; and you will come across herons, kingfishers, grebes and other creatures who like the privacy of backwaters and reedy pools.

Long Wittenham lies on a backwater of the Thames surrounded by chalk hills and has a fine old church with a sundial.

The Upper Thames – Thames Head to Oxford

The source of the Thames is a disappointing place. Thames Head is situated on the southern slope of Trewsbury Mead in the northern Cotswolds near Cirencester. Here there is a dry hole from which water dribbles on wet days. The course of the river then follows an overgrown ditch until it reaches Ashton Keynes. From Ashton Keynes to Cricklade it is possible to float a small canoe in the river, but it is not a public highway until you have reached the Half Penny Bridge at Lechlade.

The River Churn joins the Thames at Cricklade. Some people believe that the Churn is the real Thames, owing to the fact that it carries more water and that it flows through the city of

The Church of St. John the Baptist, a fine building in the perpendicular style, looks down over the wide Market Place in Cirencester.

Cirencester. Cirencester is an important town where the Romans built one of their major west of England cities. It was the crossing point of three important thoroughfares, Akeman Street, Ermine Street and Fosse Way. Cirencester was important in the Middle Ages too, and has a handsome Market Place in which stands the church of St. John the Baptist, built with money made by wealthy wool merchants.

Below Fairford, just before Lechlade, the Thames is joined by the River Coln; a very pretty river with some attractive villages along its course. The best example is Bibury, whose centre is built in Cotswold stone and which has some fine buildings, including a church and a manor house, now a hotel. By the bridge is a trout farm, with the fish swimming in a bypass of the river. In the upper reaches of the Coln you can take a minor road across to Chedworth where, among the trees, you can see one of the best examples of a Roman villa in Britain. With its luxurious baths and elaborate

*Bibury, on the River Coln, is a delightful place with Cotswold stone-built houses
and a charming row of fourteenth-century buildings called Arlington Cottages
which were converted into homes for local weavers.*

mosaic floors, it is thought that Chedworth may have been used as
a leisure centre for the officers of the Cirencester garrison.

After Lechlade, the Thames is officially navigable and the
river is full of boats and barges. From Lechlade to Teddington the
river now falls by regulated stages, controlled by weirs and locks,
but until the Thames Conservancy was formed in 1866, there was
no such system. Drops in the water level were marked by weirs,
and getting boats up or down them was an extremely hazardous
business. To add to the difficulties, the Thames water was used by
water mills, the operation of which would also cause changes in the
level of the navigable water. One of the first of the weirs and locks
is at Buscot, where you can still see the early system of water flow
control – long paddles which were lowered into the river above the
weir.

As it approaches Oxford, the Thames is joined by the
Windrush, which flows through a particularly pretty valley. The
source of the Windrush is in the hills to the south of the Cotswold
village of Broadway. A showplace of stone buildings and home of
the famous Lygon Arms, Broadway was in the centre of the
fighting during the Civil War and was occupied in turn by both
Charles I's and Cromwell's troops. From Broadway, the little
stream wends its way past villages and on through the main street
of Bourton-on-the-Water, where the green lawns on the river
banks make a popular picnic place in summer. From Bourton,
which is near the wool town of Stow-on-the-Wold, the Windrush
passes by the Barringtons, a quarry area for Cotswold stone, and
then under the old stone bridge at Burford.

Burford is a most attractive town, full of the fine stone
houses of the wool merchants of the fifteenth and sixteenth
centuries. Burford High Street climbs the southern bank of the
valley towards the main Oxford-Cheltenham road and the
Cotswold Wild Life Park, one of the best maintained parks of this
kind in Britain. Nearby, at Minster Lovell, are the ruins of a

moated manor house where Francis Lord Lovell, a supporter of Lambert Simnel, starved to death as he hid in a secret chamber.

As the Windrush heads towards Oxford it passes Stanton Harcourt, one of the many old villages around the University city. Stanton Harcourt has a Tudor gateway and the superb kitchen of the old manor house is preserved. As it approaches Oxford the Thames changes its name, for some miles, to the Isis and is joined with the Windrush. At Oxford the Isis (Thames) steals quietly past the southern edge of the city under Folly Bridge, the finishing point of Oxford University's rowing course. From here you can walk up St. Aldate's, passing Christ Church College on the right and Pembroke College on the left, to Carfax at the city centre. The High Street runs to the right, with Brasenose College and the church of St. Mary's and All Souls on the left. St. Mary's is where Archbishop Cranmer was tried in 1555. He later repudiated his recantation and was burned at the stake. There is a superb view of Oxford from the church tower.

Nearby is the round building of the Radcliffe Camera and, behind that, the Bodleian Library and the Sheldonian Theatre. You can stroll down Broad Street where Balliol and Trinity College can be seen. Beyond is St. Giles and the Martyrs' Memorial, which recalls the burning of Latimer, Ridley and Cramner, near the site of the present Ashmolean Museum.

Left: At the Sheldonian Theatre in Oxford, designed by Christopher Wren, benefactors of the University are commemorated every June.

Below: Hertford College, Oxford, has an unusual spiral tower in its quadrangle. The college has an old and new building joined by the Bridge of Sighs.

To the east, between the University city and modern Oxford, is the River Cherwell, which rises near Banbury and, after passing Magdalen College, joins the Thames at Christchurch Meadow. This large expanse of grassy land is overlooked by Oxford Cathedral, Corpus Christi and the first of the residential colleges, established in 1264, Merton.

The Lower Thames – Oxford to Windsor

From Oxford the Thames flows due south to the old wool trade town of Abingdon, once the site of an important abbey. The abbey was destroyed in the Dissolution, but the size of the remaining guildhall and guest house is evidence of its importance. Today Abingdon is a busy market town and the home of many of the scientists who work at the atomic research establishment at Harwell. It is also a good centre for visiting a number of small but enchanting old villages such as Sutton Courtenay, Steventon and East Hendred, whose buildings date back to the sixteenth century.

After Abingdon the Thames turns eastwards to its junction with the Thame, a river which runs west from the north slopes of the Chiltern Hills and through the Vale of Aylesbury. On the Thame, near the point where it joins the Thames, is the attractive abbey town of Dorchester, where the winding main street flanked by timbered houses runs by the Norman abbey church. A lovely and peaceful spot, happily now bypassed by the main road to Oxford.

The Thames heads south again towards the gap between the Chiltern Hills and the Berkshire Downs. The river valley narrows between steeply sloping wooded hills – one of the prettiest sections of the river – with a crossing point at Wallingford that has been important since Roman times. Wallingford was granted a town charter by Henry II, whose kingship was confirmed by the Treaty

Blenheim Palace, home of John Churchill, Duke of Marlborough, was built by Vanbrugh. Parliament had to vote a quarter of a million pounds to pay for it.

*St. Helen's Church, Abingdon, recalls in its name the monastery founded in the
Thames-side town and dedicated to St. Helena
in the seventh century.*

of Wallingford, and a castle (now destroyed) was built to protect
this strategic crossing. Today Wallingford is a market town and
popular rendezvous for weekend visitors.

Also in the gap between the hills are Goring, on the east bank
of the river, and its counterpart Streatley, on the west. This is the
crossing point of the Icknield Way, which spans southern England
from the Wash to the Bristol Channel. Near Streatley is the
splendid classical eighteenth-century house of Basildon Park,
which has many beautifully furnished rooms.

For those who have read *The Wind in the Willows* by Kenneth
Grahame, Pangbourne is a fascinating and evocative place to visit.
The author lived and died in Pangbourne, and the imaginative tale
of river creatures headed by Ratty, Mole and Toad, whose
adventures took place along the river between Pangbourne and
Cookham, were told to his son Alastair as bedtime stories.
Grahame was later prevailed upon to write them down; after initial
bad reviews, they became a classic of English literature. The great
hall where Toad led his bombastic existence could have been
inspired by Hardwick House or Mapledurham. At the approach to
the now very industrial town of Reading, Mapledurham is a lovely
Tudor house, open to the public. It has belonged to the Blount
family since 1588, and is one of the most interesting and well cared
for houses on the Thames. The church has an unusual division of
the aisles into Protestant and Catholic sections, for the Blounts
remained staunchly Catholic throughout the years of Catholic
persecution. In the grounds is one of the oldest working watermills
on the river.

Top: *The village of Hambledon lies about a mile inland from the Thames between Henley and Marlow in a green valley in the Chiltern Hills.*

For those who visit the river with a view to enjoying its rural beauty Reading is best passed by quickly. Beyond it, however, is the charming village of Sonning, with wooded islands around which the river plays a game of hide-and-seek. There is an old mill here which has been converted into a restaurant and theatre, attracting many people from Reading and the surrounding area. From here the Thames winds its way northwards towards the handsome town of Henley-on-Thames, home of the famous July regattas, which attract oarsmen from all over the world. The regattas began in 1839 but the history of Henley goes back much further, for it has always been an important river crossing. The bridge that stands today was built in 1786 and the parish church of St. Mary's in sixteenth century, with a chantry house dating back to the 1400's.

Beyond Henley is a straight stretch of river on which the regattas take place, but after this the river twists and turns again as it continues on its way to Mill End. Here the old mill has been converted into houses and the extensive weir provides wild waters for canoeing enthusiasts. A half mile inland from Mill End is the unspoilt village of Hambledon, with its sixteenth-century church and pleasant old pubs. The Hambledon Valley stretches inland to one of the most untouched parts of the Chiltern hills where villages like Turville and Fingest nestle under the lee of wooded hills.

The great curve of the river between Henley and Maidenhead was once an area occupied by monasteries and abbeys. At Medmenham there are the remains of an abbey attached to a house, later associated with Sir Francis Dashwood whose Hell Fire Club caused a scandal in the eighteenth century. At Hurley there are huge tithe barns of a former monastery, and at Bisham a riverside church and abbey, the latter now used as the National Sports Training Centre.

Marlow, also the site of a yearly regatta, is an idyllic riverside town. The white suspension bridge joins the Berkshire bank, on which stands the Compleat Angler Hotel, to the Buckinghamshire side, on which rises the church of All Saints. Despite the encroachment of new estates on this fast-developing part of the Thames valley, Marlow centre retains some of its old atmosphere and the High Street contains many seventeenth- and eighteenth-century buildings.

To the north of Marlow lies High Wycombe, traditionally a furniture-making town due to the abundance of beech woods in the surrounding hills. Nearby, is West Wycombe, a village of

Left: Henley has a handsome eighteenth-century bridge crossing the Thames to the High Street, with its fine church and fourteenth-century Chantry House.

Below: A white suspension bridge crosses the Thames at Marlow, flanked by All Saints Church on the north bank and the Compleat Angler Hotel on the south bank.

Above: A church with a golden ball on its tower tops the hill above West
Wycombe and the house and park of the eighteenth-century rake, Sir Francis
Dashwood.

Right: Ellesborough Church spire rises above the slopes of the Chiltern Hills
near Wendover. The Ridgeway Path follows the ridge here, providing some
superb views of the Vale of Aylesbury.

sixteenth- to eighteenth-century houses adjoining the splendid
West Wycombe House. The house and its park were owned by Sir
Francis Dashwood, who entertained Benjamin Franklin there as
well as many of his less reputable friends. Sir Francis was responsi-
ble for the unusual church built on the summit of the hill behind
West Wycombe and the mausoleum containing the tombs of the
Dashwood family. Below ground Sir Francis dug a tunnel with
various large chambers where the members of the Hell Fire Club
could carouse to their hearts' content without being disturbed.

Beyond Marlow, at Bourne End, the Thames turns south
again, passing Cookham. A village with several half-timbered
houses, Cookham was once the home of Stanley Spencer, whose
paintings hang in a brick building in the main street. The village
was the setting of many of the artist's pictures including a famous
Resurrection in which he portrayed village residents.

There is a beautiful stretch of river between Cookham and
Maidenhead, passing the Cliveden Estate and its hanging woods.
Cliveden was the home of the Astor family, one of whom was
Lady Astor, the influential politician of the 1930s whose friends
were known as the Astor Set. The house, on the site of the former
home of the Duke of Buckingham, is situated on a plateau surrounded by trees and its parterre, stretching towards the hanging

Windsor Castle, its bulk dominated by Henry II's great Round Tower, stands on a chalk cliff above the Thames and the village of Eton.

woods, offers superb views of the Thames Valley. The property belongs to the National Trust, but the house is now used as a hotel. After Cliveden Reach, the river enters Boulter's Lock, a popular riverside rendezvous in Edwardian times. Today only echoes of this colourful period remain as the river flows away under Brunel's railway bridge, portrayed by Turner in his painting, *Wind, Rain and Steam*.

From Maidenhead, although still 30 miles from the centre of London, the Thames begins to enter the outskirts of suburbia. The river traffic increases, with steamers full of people enjoying a day on the river and hired motorboats and cruisers with names like *Tahiti Princess* and *Bali Hai*. However, there are still green fields and villages to either side at Bray, and at Dorney where an Elizabethan manor and church lie in the centre of open country.

Although Windsor – once the setting for a royal hunting lodge – is now on the fringes of urban London, its royal atmosphere still prevails. The castle stands boldly on the hill above the river, and its battlements provide a splendid view of Eton College, with its fine chapel built by Henry VI as one part of a great cathedral left incomplete after he was deposed.

The Guildhall in Windsor High Street was completed by Wren and contains a portrait gallery. Behind it run cobbled Market Street and Church Lane.

Windsor is still a royal castle and the Queen's standard floats over the towers when she is in residence. Windsor Great Park, behind the castle, is a royal estate too; when great events like the Windsor Horse Show take place here, the Queen and her family attend. At Smith Lawn, in the centre of the park, Prince Charles can often be seen taking part in a polo match. The castle is divided into two wards by the great central Round Tower. In the upper ward are the Royal State Apartments, which can be visited when the Queen is not in residence. In the lower ward is St. George's Chapel, a lovely example of English Gothic architecture dedicated to the patron of the Order of the Garter.

A royal presence from the past is recreated at the now-disused railway station. Queen Victoria relives, in wax, her arrival at Windsor by train. There is a Guard of Honour waiting at the station and the strains of the nostalgic music of Empire are the background to military orders to 'present arms'. South of Windsor Great Park, the Berkshire countryside stretches towards the North Downs, but to the east the river banks are invaded by riverside suburbs where modern houses have usurped the cottages and stone churches of pre-industrial Britain.

ENGLAND'S HEARTLAND

The Midlands consists of the great inland region that lies between the Chiltern Hills, the Pennines, the River Severn and the Wash. The little town of Meriden between Birmingham and Coventry claims to be the exact centre of England, but the heart of the country resists such precise definition. In the Midland counties, with their rich agricultural soil, the great estates of the barons were established. These powerful overlords played an important part in the destiny of England between medieval times and the coming of the Industrial Revolution. It was in the Midlands that many of the decisive battles in English history were fought. In 1460 there was the Battle of Northampton, where Henry VI was taken prisoner; and at Bosworth, near Leicester, Richard III died. In 1486 Henry VII put down the Lambert Simnel rebellion at Stoke-on-Trent; and Charles I was defeated in the famous battle at Naseby by Cromwell in 1645.

The Industrial Revolution confirmed the importance of this part of the country. Coal and iron deposits between Birmingham and Manchester created new industries, and new towns were built to accommodate the expanding population. A dense network of railways and canals was developed to transport the products from new factories to other parts of Britain and to the ports from which they were shipped overseas. At the same time, new systems of farming were being evolved alongside the enclosure system of the seventeenth and eighteenth centuries, making the land more productive.

The result of these two developments in English life was to create in the Midlands a countryside of great contrasts. Large areas were given over to industry; the landscape despoiled, with factories and furnaces belching black smoke and piling up their detritus on the green hills. In other more rural areas the open-field system gave way to enclosures, imposing a chequerboard pattern on the land. In some places, however, the land was unsuitable for farming and, in areas like the Peak District of Derbyshire, the countryside retained its natural appearance.

Today, the visitor to the Midlands may be very pleasantly

Anne Hathaway lived in this thatched cottage at Shottery, near Stratford-upon-Avon, until she married Shakespeare. Some of the furnishings, that one can see today, including a four-poster bed, belonged to her.

surprised for, in this centre of industry, there is much natural beauty along the rivers and canals and on the hills. A fascinating historic presence can be seen in the castles and manor houses that still survive from Tudor times onwards. There is also a great deal to interest the industrial archaeologist, looking back with curiosity at the century that made modern Britain, seen in old railways, bridges, canals and deserted industrial buildings of many years ago.

The Course of the Trent

The River Trent curves round the northern Midlands like a garland. It begins life as a small stream near Stoke-on-Trent and flows south from the capital of the pottery towns, Stafford, and into the green Valley of Trent. From here, it begins its slow northward progress through Nottinghamshire to the River Humber.

At Stoke-on-Trent – a confederation of the leading pottery towns, Burslem, Fenton, Hanley, Longton and Tunstall, which Arnold Bennett wrote about in his novels – the Trent flows through a land of clay which was used for pottery as long ago as the Bronze Age. Pottery artefacts from the Bronze Age and Roman times can be seen at the Hanley City Museum. Pottery-making as an industry did not, however, begin until the seventeenth century when local potters perceived that the presence of coal and the minerals used in the glazing process in the same area as the clay could be a basis for the manufacture of pottery on a large scale. The founder of the industry was Josiah Wedgwood. In 1759 he set out to manufacture pottery that could be produced in large quantities and sold cheaply to the increasing population of the Midlands. He was soon followed by others, among them Josiah Spode and Thomas Minton who, like Wedgwood, imprinted their unmistakable style on the products they made.

To the south of Stoke-on-Trent the river flows into the Trent Valley, where it is joined by the River Sow. The Sow passes through Stafford, where the streets still follow the medieval street plan of the town. There are several old timbered houses in Stafford and among the older mansions is the High House where Charles I and his general, Prince Rupert, stayed in 1642. This was the time when the first encounters between Royalists and Cromwellian troops were taking place and the indecisive Battle of Edge Hill was fought near Banbury. Another famous resident of Stafford was Izaak Walton, who was born in Eastgate Street. Later, he moved to a cottage in nearby Shallowford which is now an Izaak Walton Museum.

The region round Stafford is idyllic, with the woods of Cannock Chase on the southern slopes of the valley. Further south, in stark contrast, are Birmingham and Wolverhampton, surrounded by the area once known as the Black Country. Thanks to modern attitudes to industrial development and new techniques in dealing with smoke and debris from factories and furnaces, the Black Country no longer deserves such a forbidding name. Though still a place of industry, the area surrounding Wolverhampton has some attractive countryside and interesting buildings to offer. Himley, five miles south of Wolverhampton, is a rural spot on the banks of the Staffordshire and Worcestershire Canal. Along the canal, to the north, are Wightwick Manor, with its collection of William Morris papers and Pre-Raphaelite paintings;

*The three spires of Lichfield Cathedral, known as the Ladies of the Vale,
dominate the tranquil cathedral close with its medieval houses.*

and Moseley Old Hall, an Elizabethan mansion where Charles II
hid after his defeat at the Battle of Worcester in 1651.

Wolverhampton lies to the west and adjoins the sprawling
conglomerate of Birmingham. To the north lies Lichfield, with its
lovely three-spired church in the midst of fourteenth- and
fifteenth-century houses. Dr. Johnson was born in this city and his
house in Breadmarket Street is a museum to him and his bio-
grapher, Boswell. These two men are the subject of statues which
stand in the market square. Other famous residents of the cathedral
city were David Garrick, the actor, and Elias Ashmole, the antiquarian whose collection formed the basis of the Ashmolean
Museum at Oxford.

The River Trent flows east to the north of Lichfield and then, past the pretty village of Alrewas, turns towards Burton-upon-Trent – a town famous for its beer, first brewed by Benedictine monks in the Middle Ages.

At Nottingham, home of Nottingham Castle which has the old pub Trip to Jerusalem embedded in the castle rock, the Trent enters a county remarkable for the great variety of its landscape. To the west of the city are the coalfields which D. H. Lawrence used as a background for many of his novels. To the north is Sherwood Forest, fictional home of Robin Hood and his Merry Men, who robbed the rich to feed the poor – constantly defying the wicked Sheriff of Nottingham.

As the Trent flows north it passes the gaunt ruins of Newark Castle where King John died in 1216. The castle was destroyed after three sieges by Cromwell's troops during the Civil War. As it heads towards the Humber, the river passes through flat Lincolnshire countryside and past Gainsborough, a busy market town. Here you can see the Old Hall, the largest medieval house in England where both Richard III and Henry VIII were once guests.

Wollaton Hall, near Nottingham, is a Renaissance tour de force built by Sir Francis Willoughby. It is now a natural history museum and has a fine park with perhaps the first glass house to have been built in England.

The Derwent river flows through a narrow valley at Matlock, a spa surrounded
by high tors, on one of which is nineteenth-century Riber Castle.

Derby and The Peaks

Derby is an industrial centre associated with Rolls-Royce and
Crown Derby Pottery. Nonetheless, the city still retains many old
buildings – reminders of its past as a market town. The sixteenth-
century church of All Saints contains the tomb of Bess of
Hardwick, Countess of Shrewsbury. She was the influential wife
of the Fourth Duke of Shrewsbury who built or rebuilt a number
of local manor houses including Hardwick Hall and Chatsworth.
To the north of Derby are two important mansions. One is
Kedleston Hall, a classical eighteenth-century building erected for
the Curzon family by James Paine and Robert Adam; the other, in
the Erewash valley to the east, is the Old Hall at Little Hallam.

To the west and north of Derby lie the beautiful Derby
Dales, where the rivers Dove, Derwent and Wye cut through
limestone rock to create secluded valleys and gorges. In the
Derwent Valley is Matlock, a spa in Victorian times. Matlock is
surrounded by steep hills and cliffs rising to High Tor and to the
Heights of Abraham (which were given their name by an officer
who served with Woolfe at Quebec). Near Matlock, in a valley on
the east bank of the river, is Crich. Here you will find an unusual
tram museum in a disused quarry, with tracks on which these
quaint old vehicles go through their paces.

The most famous of the Derby Dales is Dovedale, an un-
usually lovely valley with a narrow gorge, high pinnacles of rock
and abundant vegetation along its floor. The gorge is about two
miles long and makes a delightful walk.

Above: The Dovedale Gorge, with its wooded bed and green slopes climbing up to bare crags, is one of the most picturesque spots in the Peak District National Park.

Right: The River Wye flows under a 700-year-old bridge at Bakewell, an attractive town among the wooded hills of the Peak District.

To the north of the Dales are the foothills of the High Peaks, where a wild section of countryside is hemmed in by the industrial conurbations of Manchester and Sheffield. Here, near the source of the River Dove at Axe Edge, is Buxton where warm mineral springs bubble to the surface and have been providing visitors with health-giving baths since the time of the Romans. The springs were popularized by the Fifth Duke of Devonshire, descendant of Bess of Hardwick. The Duke built the elegant Georgian Crescent in front of St. Anne's Well, facing the green slopes leading up to Hardwick Mount. To the right of the Crescent the Pavilion Gardens stretch along the River Wye and contain a complex of buildings including an opera house, theatre and concert hall as well as the mineral baths.

From Buxton the River Wye runs south to Bakewell – home of the Bakewell Tart – a pleasant town of stone houses with a museum in the Old House. Near Bakewell, also on the River Wye, is Haddon Hall, a well-maintained medieval house with a romantic history. Dorothy Vernon, daughter of the house, eloped with Sir John Manners. Among its features, Haddon Hall has a fine banqueting hall and a seventeenth-century long-gallery with views across the Wye Valley. Nearby is Chatsworth House, built by the Duke of Devonshire. This Palladian palace is decorated with many ceiling paintings and houses some portraits of the Devonshire family, including some by Van Dyck. Mary Queen of Scots was a frequent visitor here while she was in captivity under the care of the Duke of Shrewsbury, husband of Bess of Hardwick. George II died at Chatsworth and his body was laid out in the State Room.

The glorious hilly country of the Peak District lies to the north. High rocky crags rise above moorlands, and deep caverns in the limestone rock provide adventurous exploration for speleologists. From Chatsworth the approach to the High Peaks is via the Derwent Valley, past a number of pretty villages like Baslow.

Bottom: Chatsworth was begun in 1687 by William Cavendish who became the 1st Duke of Devonshire. The architects were William Talman and Thomas Archer.

At the eastern end of the Hope Valley the road leads to Grindleford where the Longshaw Estate, famous for its sheep dog trials, is situated. Nearby is the village of Hethersage which has two claims to fame, though both may be fictional. It is said that Robin Hood's Little John is buried in the churchyard here and that Hethersage was the setting for Charlotte Brontë's *Jane Eyre*, North Lee Hall being the Manor House in the novel.

Further up the Hope Valley is a turning to Bamford and Ladybower reservoir; but straight ahead lies Castleton, the centre of the cave district of the peaks. Above the village stands the stark ruin of Peveril Castle which was built by Richard Peveril in 1176. At the foot of the slopes leading up to the castle is the Peak Cavern, which tunnels under the limestone ridge for about quarter of a mile. Further up the valley is the Speedwell Mine where you can travel along the tunnels of the mine by water for about half a mile – an impressive journey ending in a huge pothole chamber, the height of which has never been established. Castleton is surrounded by steep, grass-covered slopes and rocky outcrops. At Edale there is a centre for adventure holidays where you can spend a week or two rock-climbing, hang-gliding, pot-holing or participating in other energetic activities under the watchful eyes of experienced instructors.

From their northern heights, the High Peaks slope rapidly down to the great industrial plexus of England, across which sprawl the cities of Manchester, Huddersfield, Leeds and Sheffield – the centres of British industrial power in the nineteenth century.

The ancient art of thatching is still practised in the English countryside. This thatcher is rebuilding a roof at Bidford-on-Avon in Worcestershire.

Shakespeare and his family are buried in Holy Trinity Church, whose elegant
spire rises by the quiet waters of the Avon in Stratford-upon-Avon.

Shakespeare Country and the Rural Midlands

To the south and west of Birmingham the countryside holds its
own against the tide of industry. Around the cities of Coventry,
Leicester and Northampton rural life is still preserved, though the
farming methods now used are more productive than those in
operation before the days of scientific agriculture. To the south of
Birmingham, in Warwickshire, Shakespeare Country stretches
from the Forest of Arden to Stratford-upon-Avon; a lovely rolling
countryside of green meadows, woods and rippling streams which
is the inspiration and setting for such comedies as *As You like It* and
A Midsummer Night's Dream.

This gentle countryside is well-watered by rivers, and
crossed by the canals which were built by Thomas Telford to
provide a cheap system of transport for the goods produced in
Midlands' industrial towns. Today these canals are used for leisure
rather than commerce and there is no better way to see the
southern Midland counties than from a cruiser or narrow boat.

The most famous waterway of all is the River Avon, which
rises in Naseby in Leicestershire and enters the Bristol Channel at
Avonmouth near Bristol, passing through Shakespeare's birthplace on the way. Athough Stratford-upon-Avon receives more
visitors than any other town in the Midlands, it has managed to
preserve the atmosphere of a market town. In its centre, old brick
and timbered houses converted into shops, restaurants and cafes,
line the streets. Along the river, past the Shakespeare Memorial

New Place, the house to which Shakespeare retired in Stratford, and where he died, was torn down, but the garden remains.

Theatre, is the peaceful haven of Holy Trinity Church where Shakespeare, his wife Anne, and eldest daughter Susanna are buried. The broken font is the one at which Shakespeare was baptized.

The house in which Shakespeare was born is in Henley Street; a comfortable, half-timbered building furnished in Elizabethan style, with a garden full of the plants mentioned in Shakespeare's plays. Having become a successful playwright in London, Shakespeare returned to his home town. In 1611 he bought a house at New Place in Chapel Street, but enjoyed only 5 years there before he died in 1616 at the age of 52. At the corner of Henley Street and High Street is the house of Judith Quiney, Shakespeare's youngest daughter, which is now used as an information centre. Further along High Street is Harvard House where Katherine Rogers – mother of John Harvard, founder of Harvard University – lived.

There are other places near Stratford-upon-Avon that have strong Shakespearian connections. Shottery, two miles away, was the home of Shakespeare's wife, Anne Hathaway, the daughter of a rich farmer. The cottage was damaged by fire in 1969 but has been completely restored and, with its garden, evokes a picture of sixteenth-century country life at a time when the whole population of England was barely more than eight million. A short distance from Shottery is Wilmcote, where the house of Mary Arden, Shakespeare's mother, can be seen. This is a typical Tudor farmhouse and many items of farming equipment from that time

The Earl of Leicester converted these houses in Warwick belonging to religious guilds into a haven for poor brethren now called Lord Leycester's Hospital.

are on show in the outbuildings. Two miles east is Charlecote Park, where the young Shakespeare got into trouble for poaching deer.

North-east of Stratford lies Warwick, with its massive castle rising high above the River Avon. Under the Earls of Warwick, this was the centre of power for a long period of English history. One of these Warwick nobles was the Duke of Clarence, who was drowned in a butt of Malmsey wine according to Shakespeare's play, *Richard III*. An even more unpleasant end came to John Dudley, Earl of Warwick. After attempting to put Lady Jane Grey on the English throne in the place of Mary Tudor, he died on the executioner's block. Warwick Castle now belongs to Madame Tussaud's and wax-works add to the forbidding atmosphere of this grim fortress. A collection of torture instruments on display act as a reminder of the fate that awaited those who incurred the wrath of the powerful barons. Much of Warwick caught on fire in 1694, but some of the old buildings survived. The Norman church of St. Mary is where the first Earls of Warwick, the Beauchamp family, have their family chapel. The Lord Leychester Hospital was founded by Robert Dudley, a favourite of Elizabeth I's, for soldiers wounded in the Queen's service.

On the east bank of the Avon, adjoining Warwick, is Royal Leamington Spa. It acquired its Royal prefix in 1838 when Queen Victoria approved its health-giving waters. These flow from underground springs and are piped into the Pump Room which, even today, is attended by many sufferers from rheumatic ailments. Like many spas, Leamington has a dignified and sedate appearance and it has many fine Georgian houses along its wide, tree-lined streets.

To the north of Warwick another great castle rears its ruined battlements. Kenilworth was the centre of baronial power in an earlier age when John of Gaunt, the fourth son of Edward III, ruled the area. His great banqueting hall can still be discovered among the ruins. Robert Dudley, who became Earl of Leicester entertained Queen Elizabeth I here and the gardens he created are still visible.

To the north lies Coventry, the phoenix city which rose from the ashes left by a German air raid in the Second World War. It incorporated its ruined cathedral into a new, imaginative concept which draws visitors from all over the world to see the architecture of Sir Basil Spence and works of art by such modern masters as Graham Sutherland and John Piper. The bombs did not, however, destroy everything in Coventry. The city still possesses a number of interesting old buildings including St. Mary's Hall and the church of the Holy Trinity. Even more indestructible is the legend of Lady Godiva, who rode naked through the town in protest against heavy taxes imposed by her husband – an Earl of Mercia. She is commemorated by a statue which stands in Broadgate.

East lies the rich countryside of Leicestershire and Northamptonshire, crossed by the rivers Welland and Nene. This is farming and fox-hunting country in which many fine mansions can be found. One is Kirby Hall which, with its ruined façade, evokes the sixteenth century and the days of Mary Queen of Scots. This tragic Queen was imprisoned and executed at Fotheringay Castle, nearby. Only a mound remains of the castle, but its fine

Fotheringay Church stands by the River Nene near the site of the now-demolished castle where Mary Queen of Scots was imprisoned and executed.

Farnborough Hall is an Italianate mansion near Edge Hill, where one of the major battles between the Parliamentarians and Royalists took place in 1642.

church can still be seen by the banks of the River Nene. Another imposing house is Castle Ashby, to the east of Northampton. Built in 1574 by the first Earl of Northampton, it is owned by the Compton family who have held the estate for over 400 years.

The country between Northampton and Leicester is rich in agricultural lands which stretch north to Melton Mowbray and incorporates what once was Rutland, the smallest county in England (now a part of Leicestershire). This is the centre of traditional English country life, with its three famous hunts – the Quorn, the Cottesmore and the Belvoir – meeting in the area. The famous Belvoir foxhounds are named after the castle, an eleventh-century fortress built by the standard bearer of William the Conqueror. Belvoir was taken over by the Manners family, who became the Dukes of Rutland, and their descendants still own the castle today.

From here to the east the Leicestershire Wolds, which give variety to the landscape of the Belvoir Valley, gradually decline toward the flat lands of the Fens.

THE BORDER COUNTRIES

FRONTIER TOWNS
—— AMONG THE ——
ORCHARDS

The counties on the borders of Wales, watered by the rivers Severn, Wye and Dee, have a romantic atmosphere which has inspired poets and musicians. A. E. Housman reflected this countryside in his poem *A Shropshire Lad*, and Elgar, who lived in the Malvern Hills, drew from much of his environment melodies which express the very essence of the spirit of rural England.

In the valleys of Gloucester and Hereford and Worcester the romantic atmosphere is particularly strong in springtime when the apple orchards are in bloom with pink and white blossoms and the hedgerows are bursting into leaf. Tranquility and stability are the hallmark of the border counties, the villages of timbered houses and the towns of Cotswold stone give a feeling of continuity to the life of the countryside and the ruined castles, adding a picturesque touch to the landscape, are now only a glorious reminder of the embattled years when Great Britain was becoming a unified kingdom.

The southern half of the counties that border on Wales are in the river systems of the Wye and Severn both of which spring from the mountains of Plynlimon in central Wales but wend their separate ways to the mouth of the Severn. The Wye flowing south to Builth Wells, and known as Afon Gwy, enters England at Hay-on-Wye and the Severn, curving north through Welshpool, passes through Shrewsbury before turning south for its journey to the Bristol Channel.

As it enters the Channel the Severn becomes a wide estuary separating the Welsh county of Gwent from the English one of Avon to which it is joined by a graceful and busy suspension bridge built in 1966, which connects southern Wales to the M4 motorway to London and the M5 to the north of England.

The northern border county of Cheshire is watered by the River Dee which starts its life at Lake Bala, as the Afon Dyfrdwy, and emerges into England through the lovely Vale of Llangollen. It then meanders gently through Chester on the Cheshire plain to the estuary of the Dee between the Clwydian mountains and the flat peninsula of the Wirral.

The Malvern Hills rise gently above the Worcestershire countryside and contain many natural springs, round which grew fashionable spas.

Around the Severn Valley

Even in the days when trade with America was in its infancy, Bristol, which was reached through Avonmouth on the mouth of the Severn, was England's most important port. From here John Cabot and his son, Sebastian, set off to discover the mainland of North America in 1497, a year before his fellow Genoese, Christopher Columbus, landed in mainland America. But before this, merchant venturers were already exploring the world and Bristol had become important as a trading centre through which passed wool from the Cotswolds and wine from Portugal and Spain. The discovery and colonization of America gave the port new impetus as the products of the New World, tobacco, potatoes, leather, cotton, timber and spices began to arrive and slave labourers were exported.

The focal point of Bristol's activity, then as now, was the floating harbour, an artificial dock, now partially filled in, on the banks of which Robert, Earl of Gloucester, built a castle in 1126. Here the docksides were packed with sailing ships and Corn Street was crowded with merchants and agents making deals and paying 'on the nail', the flat-topped pillars in the streets on which was placed the money confirming business transactions. The meeting place of the merchants, traders and sailors as well as the prostitutes and entertainers who frequented the port was King Street, where the Llandoger Trow, a seventeenth-century inn, is still in business.

The end of the slave trade diminished the profits of the port but new attempts to remain ahead of competitors, like Liverpool, came with the development of steam driven ships. One of these, The *Great Britain*, built in Bristol by Isambard Kingdom Brunel, made its maiden voyage to New York in 1845 and lies today in Bristol's Wapping dock.

To the west of this area lies Bristol's cathedral, founded as an Augustinian abbey in 1148 and added to and rebuilt in later centuries. Of the original building, only the chapter house, the south transept and the east walk of the cloister survive, but other early thirteenth- to fifteenth-century parts of the building are also incorporated into the fabric of the church, notably the east window of the Lady chapel, the choir, and the elder Lady chapel on the left of the north transept entrance. An interesting item is the tablet to Hakluyt, the chronicler of the early voyages of English seamen, who was prebendary at Bristol in the sixteenth century.

To the east of the harbour is St. Mary's Radcliffe, a fourteenth-century church, which Queen Elizabeth I described as 'the fairest in England', and where there is an effigy of the Queen and the tomb of William Penn, father of the founder of Pennsylvania. Near the church is the house of Thomas Chatterton, the brilliant but tragic poet who poisoned himself in London, and further west near the junction of the River Avon and the floating harbour, is Temple Meads station.

To the north of the floating harbour the city stretches up to the hills where the University and the City Art Gallery and Art Museum stand. Beyond them lies Clifton, a residential area with once opulent eighteenth- and early nineteenth-century mansions. From the heights of Clifton a suspension bridge, designed by Brunel, crosses the Clifton Gorge through which shipping threads its way to and from Avonmouth and the open sea.

Following the course of the River Avon to the east you come to Bath, the most elegant Georgian city in England whose thermal

The handsome city of Bath contains some of the finest Georgian architecture in England as well as the best preserved Roman baths.

waters have made it a popular spa since Roman times. According to legend the medicinal qualities of the waters were discovered by King Bladud, father of King Lear, who having contracted a leprous disease along with his herd of swine, recovered by rolling with them in the warm muddy waters of the pools. The Roman baths were unearthed in the eighteenth-century and lie alongside the Pump Room built in 1796 on the site of the rooms which Beau Nash, the famous Master of Ceremonies of the spa, made fashionable at the beginning of that century.

The beau monde of Nash's day was provided with a city worthy of it by John Wood, an admirer of the Italian architect Palladio. Wood (who arrived in Bath in 1727) and his son almost rebuilt the previously medieval town, transforming it into the elegant showplace whose finest features are the Queen Square, the Royal Crescent, the Assembly Rooms and the Pulteney Bridge, which was designed by Robert Adam in 1770. Inevitably, a fashionable holiday and curative centre like Bath was bound to attract many writers, and the city appears in the books of Tobias Smollett, Henry Fielding and in Jane Austen's *Northanger Abbey* and *Persuasion* and Charles Dickens' *Pickwick Papers*.

In the wooded hills around Bath are numerous lovely villages built of Cotswold stone, with fine manor houses as well as more humble but no less attractive cottages. One of these splendid early nineteenth-century houses is at Claverton, and is occupied by the American Museum, founded in 1861 by two American bene-factors; another is at Combe Hay, a manor house with a fine garden and ornamental lake. And there is Midford Castle, shaped like a clover leaf, near Monkton Combe.

The tower of Bath Abbey rises above the baths, which the Romans called Aquae
Sulis after a Celtic goddess, and which became the centre of the town spa.

The Vale of Berkeley to the north of Bath is penned in
between the Severn and the Cotswolds, a flat alluvial plain where
there are two features of considerable interest. One of these is the
Slimbridge Wild Fowl Trust Reserve, where Sir Peter Scott,
naturalist and artist, provides a sanctuary for water fowl; the other
is Berkeley Castle. This feudal fortress built in the twelfth century
was the scene of one of the most brutal murders of an English king,
when in 1327 Edward II was killed by having hot irons passed
through his body. A pleasanter picture of Berkeley is evoked in the
parish church, where Edward Jenner, discoverer of the smallpox
vaccination which has saved millions of lives, is buried in the
chancel.

On the west side of the Severn facing the vale of Berkeley is
the Forest of Dean, a vast 27,000-acre area rich in wild life. Here
the rights of miners to dig free coal from the seams that lie under
the trees and of quarrymen to cut stone, are still preserved. This
area stretches across to the River Wye on which lies Tintern Abbey
in a superb wooded gorge.

The River Wye begins its journey to join the Severn in Central Wales and crosses into England after leaving the Welsh village of Hay-on-Wye, where scores of bookshops line the pretty village streets around the old castle. The green valley of the Wye, like that of the River Dove which flows through the Golden Valley a few miles to the south, is typical of much of the pastoral countryside along the Welsh borders.

Hereford lies along the Wye valley, a bustling market town and centre of the Hereford cattle industry, but once a frontier town protected against the Welsh by a wall, the remains of which can be seen near the Wye bridge. Around the cathedral, which is situated in a pleasant open space, there are a number of interesting buildings including the Bishop's Palace, near the river, and in Gwynne Street, alongside the palace, the house where Nell Gwynne, mistress of Charles II was born. David Garrick the famous eighteenth-century actor was also born in Hereford in the house in Widemarsh Street that is now the Raven Inn.

From Hereford the Wye flows through some very pretty countryside, passing through Ross-on-Wye, which is perched attractively on a spur of hill above the river, and meanders down to Goodrich Castle, an imposing strongpoint set above the gorge and with fine views down the valley. The castle was owned by a Royalist supporter and was captured by Cromwell's troops in

Overleaf: The River Wye meanders gently across the broad, green valley below Ross-on-Wye, an attractive old town on the fringes of the Welsh Black Mountains.

Below: Berkeley Castle, the feudal stronghold where Edward II was murdered, also has its gentler side here in the Old Bowling Alley, now a terrace walk.

When the Gloucester-Sharpness Canal was built in 1827 it turned the medieval cathedral city and former wool town of Gloucester into an important riverside port.

1646. To the south of Goodrich lies the most sublime part of the Wye valley as the river plunges through a wooded gorge to Symonds Yat, from the top of which there is a panoramic view of the valley. There is a hotel at the bottom of the gorge and from its terraces you can enjoy a view of the river and the sheer slope of Symonds Yat Rock.

South of Symonds Yat the river flows into Monmouth where it is joined by the Monnow river. The town has an eleventh-century castle where Henry V was born and an unusual Norman fortified bridge whose gatehouse was built in 1260. From here the River Wye flows down to Chepstow on the mouth of the Severn, which broadens out from the river a few miles south of the city of Gloucester.

Gloucester is a busy and thriving town which has been much rebuilt and expanded to cope with its commercial development but its cathedral, built in 1092, has remained unchanged since its handsome Norman tower was rebuilt in the fifteenth century. The cathedral became a place of pilgrimage when the tomb of Edward II, who was murdered at Berkeley Castle, was erected in the church by Edward III. Near the Vale of Gloucester, in which the cathedral city lies, the northern slopes of the Cotswolds rise steeply and at their foot is Cheltenham, a gracious spa built largely in the Regency period but with none of the raffishness associated with the Prince who built the Brighton Pavilion. Cheltenham is a decorous town which came into prominence when George III began to take the waters there and was followed by the Duke of Wellington, who hoped the waters, which contain magnesium, sodium sulphites and bicarbonate, would cure his liver complaint.

Lower Brockhampton Manor is an attractive medieval house near the village of Bromyard, in Herefordshire. The many half-timbered houses are evidence of its medieval status.

The social centre of the spa was the Pittville Pump Room built in 1825, where the medicinal waters can still be taken today, as well as at the Town Hall. Another hall which dispensed the waters was the Rotunda, but this is now the hall of a large bank. From the Rotunda there is a splendid avenue bordered by trees and statues based on those of the Athenian Erechtheion. This leads into the Promenade, the centrepiece of which is a fountain that echoes the famous Trevi fountain of Rome.

Today Cheltenham still manages to retain the air of gracious gentility which it acquired in the nineteenth century and its image is reflected in the various festivals of music, literature and dancing that take place during the summer.

To the north of Cheltenham in the Malvern Hills lies another famous spa region whose spring water attracted Victorian visitors and today Malvern Water is bottled and sold worldwide. There are several spas in the hills all named Malvern but with various qualifying adjectives, Great, Little etc. Malvern Wells, one of the smallest is where the composer Edward Elgar is buried in St. Wulstan's churchyard. This most English of all composers, who was largely self taught, gained his inspiration from the hills which he used to walk in while working out his compositions, most of which express in sound a vivid picture of the peaceful Severn countryside.

Worcester lies along the Severn to the north of the Malvern Hills and is a city known worldwide for its delicate china and, more prosaically, for its Worcestershire Sauce, the name of which is largely unpronounceable to foreign tongues. The cathedral, which was built between the eleventh and fourteenth centuries, overlooks the river and is the impressive centrepiece of Worcester. It contains the tomb of King John above which is the oldest carved royal effigy in England, and the Prince Arthur Chantry built by Henry VII to commemorate his son, Arthur. Below ground is the Norman crypt, built by St. Wulstan, in which a ceremony is held annually on the anniversary of Wulstan's death.

Worcester was a Royalist town and hid Charles II after his defeat at the battle of Worcester. The house in which he stayed, known as King Charles House, is now a restaurant. Statues of the king and his father, Charles I, stand outside the Guildhall in the centre of the town and there is a head of Cornwall, nailed by the ears to a doorway.

Below: Worcester was once a wool town but later became the headquarters of the Worcester china industry. The cathedral dates from the eleventh century.

Bottom: This iron bridge, which gave its name to the town on the Severn, was designed by F. Pritchard and cast in the foundry of Abraham Darby.

The seventeenth-century Feathers Inn at Ludlow is a fine example of the
timbered façades found in Salop and the Welsh border counties.

To the north of Worcester lies a countryside whose beauty is
in sharp contrast to the Black Country and its industrial conurbations which lie further inland to the north-east. In this corner of
the county of Hereford and Worcester there are no factor chimneys
but orchards and dairy farms flourish and there are woodlands and
hills, manor houses and castles to explore.

At Droitwich, some 9 miles to the north-east of Worcester,
there is a spa where Georgian houses are a reminder that this was an
elegant leisure centre of the world of fashion in the eighteenth
century. Further north is Hartlebury Castle, once the home of the
Bishops of Worcester and now the location of the Worcestershire
County Museum. Near Hartlebury the River Stour, which flows
through Kidderminster, a carpet-making town, joins the Severn at
Stourport-on-Severn, a town which developed during the nineteenth century when a canal from the industrial towns to the north
made it an important centre of waterway transport.

The country to the west of Worcester is purely agricultural,
especially the valley of the River Teme, a tributary of the Severn
which flows from the Welsh hills near Newtown and through
Ludlow. Ludlow castle is the most important and most formidable

Coalport china, which was popular in the eighteenth and early nineteenth centuries, was made at this kiln near Ironbridge.

castle of the border counties. This sandstone fortress which dominates the river, was built in the eleventh century by the Earl of Shrewsbury and was used and strengthened by English kings until Tudor times. The sons of Edward IV, the princes murdered in the Tower of London, were sent here for their protection; later Henry VIII's eldest brother Arthur stayed here with his wife, Katharine of Aragon (whom Henry married on Arthur's death).

To the north of Ludlow there is some very attractive countryside in which lies Stokesay Castle and the villages of Craven Arms and Church Stretton. Curving to the east is the long ridge of Wenlock Edge beyond which is Bridgenorth, a town on two levels, one on a ridge and the other by the Severn, joined by a

The Wrekin, (404m; 1,334ft high) is the cone of an extinct volcano which rises out of the Salop countryside, offering good views all round.

---

funicular railway and a winding road. There was once a castle on the site of the High Town but all that now remains is a tower in the public park. Following the road north from Ludlow you pass a hill called the Long Mynd, a popular holiday area for those who enjoy the open air. The road then carries on to Shrewsbury.

The Severn makes a protective loop around Shrewsbury which was the centre of operations against the Welsh in the twelfth and thirteenth centuries. In Edward's time there was a castle where the borough council chamber now stands near the station, at the narrow entrance to the town centre. Near the entrance to Castle Hill is the half-timbered seventeenth-century gateway to the Council House but unfortunately the Raven Hotel, where the playwright George Farquhar wrote the play *The Recruiting Officer* about Shrewsbury life in the time of Charles II, has been demolished. Further along on Pride Hill, where the post office now stands, is the place where Hotspur, the hot-headed Percy of Northumberland was hanged, drawn and quartered after having fallen prisoner to Henry IV at the battle of Shrewsbury. To the left of the post office down Mary's Street is the Guildhall and the Olde House where Mary Tudor stayed; across the river is the Abbey Church.

In the centre of the town in the square is the old market hall, an Elizabethan building, and a statue of Clive of India, who was M.P. for Shrewsbury and who lived at College Hill. The busy High Street runs along the north side of the square and has some half-timbered houses notably Ireland's Mansion and Owen's Mansion.

The south-west side of the town round which the river makes a tight loop, is devoted to parks and playing fields, one of these, called the Quarry, is overlooked by the New Church of St. Chad, an unusual round building erected by Thomas Telford, perhaps under the influence of Palladian villa architecture. Modern Shrewsbury has spread outside the old town towards the flat agricultural plain which rises in the north to join the land that separates the valley of the Severn from that of the River Dee.

To the west of Shrewsbury lies rich farmland watered by the River Tern and crossed by the Shropshire Union Canal, which once served the industrial towns further inland but is now used for pleasure boating. In the north-east is Market Drayton, a busy town with Georgian buildings and a church with a Norman tower from which there are fine views of the Tern valley, a landscape well known to Clive of India who was born here. The Tern joins the Severn at Atcham, a pretty village with a fine estate, Attingham Park, whose garden was laid out by Humphrey Repton. To the east of Atcham rises the Wrekin, a conical hill which rises

Knutsford, a quiet old Cheshire town with timbered houses and an eighteenth-century church, was the setting for Mrs. Gaskell's novel Cranford.

dramatically out of the flat farmlands of the Severn valley. Further east are several interesting villages: Shifnal has several half-timbered houses and impressed Charles Dickens, who used it as a setting for scenes in *The Old Curiosity Shop*. He also described Tong in the same book, a village near Boscobel House in whose garden is an oak descended from the one in which Charles II hid after the battle of Worcester in 1651. Another country house near the Wrekin is Weston Park at Weston-under-Lizard, the fine park-lands here were laid out by that wizard of garden landscapers, Capability Brown.

As the Dee wriggles across the Cheshire plain it traverses an area once known for salt mines, which caused much subsidence in villages and under roads; indeed, motorists may still find warnings of distorted road surfaces. The real wealth of this plain is, however, its rich farmland where cattle are fattened and crops grow abundantly around little villages with houses whose timbers are sharply defined in black and white. In the plain are slight eminences with castles on the top as on the Peckerton Hill near Tarporley, where Beeston Castle looks out over the plain, or Helsby Hill, once an Iron Age camp, which has fine views over the Mersey and the Liverpool docks.

The black and white half-timbered house with white plaster between the painted timbers is almost the trademark of Cheshire. At Knutsford off the M6 motorway the narrow streets are bordered by them and provided the background to Mrs. Gaskell's novel *Cranford*. The author was married at the parish church and is buried in its graveyard. All this north-east area of Cheshire is rich in great estates and houses.

Just to the north of Knutsford is an exceptional estate, Tatton Park, which has a nineteenth-century house by Wyatt. The Tatton estate covers some 1,000 acres and includes a deer park and garden with a Shinto temple and Japanese garden. On the fringes of Manchester, near Altrincham, is Dunham Massey, which is

Dunham Massey, the seat of the Earl of Stamford, is a classical-style building in a fine park where herds of deer roam.

surrounded by a park where herds of fallow deer roam. The house which was rebuilt in the eighteenth century is furnished in the style of the period and contains many family portraits including one of the unhappy Lady Jane Grey.

Near Stockport is Bramall Hall, one of the finest half-timbered houses in Cheshire which dates from the late sixteenth century but was restored by the Davenport family in the nineteenth century and is in superb condition. It is surrounded by a 62-acre park. A very different point of interest is the Quarry Bank Mill at Stryal. This is a restored factory community of the Industrial Revolution and reflects the paternalistic spirit of some of the nineteenth-century industrialists who built complete villages for their workforce. Quarry Bank Mill was built by Samuel Greg, a pioneer of the factory system in the cotton industry and includes housing, a school, a chapel and all the other essentials of a village, including a park. The Mill itself is in operation as a working museum where spinning and weaving techniques are demonstrated and displays tell the story of the Gregs and the community they built.

Westwards across Cheshire are the farmlands watered by the Rivers Weaver and Dare and on the borders of Wales is the River Dee which flows through Chester, the most beautifully preserved city in England, whose medieval half-timbered buildings are enclosed in a strong Roman and medieval wall.

Chester was, from AD 60 until the Romans left it in AD 380, the most powerful camp in north-east England and headquarters of the Twentieth Legion. Successive waves of pillaging Danes and Saxons destroyed the Roman city, however, and drove out most of the inhabitants. But in the tenth century a new wall was erected on the Roman foundations and life returned to the city which was rebuilt with many of the buildings we see today. Of the Roman remains still visible are parts of the city wall and an amphitheatre measuring 96×87 m (314×286 ft) outside the city walls by Newgate.

The pride of Chester is The Rows, two streets which lie between Eastgate and Newgate and are lined by timbered buildings dating back to the fourteenth century, which have a distinctive double tier of arcades and very decorative fronts in white plaster and black timber beams. The walkways of these old buildings are the busiest part of Chester for the smartest shops lie along them and the city block inside The Rows contains a modern shopping precinct.

Chester Cathedral lies within the city walls to the north of The Rows and is a beautiful red sandstone building built between Norman and Tudor times and embodying various styles of architecture. The façade has a fine Perpendicular window but it is outshone by the interior which is in Decorative and Perpendicular style and has a beautiful fourteenth-century carved wooden choir. The design of the nave and transept is interesting for the south transept is the same width as the nave while the north transept is small and flanked by the cloister and chapter houses and the monks' refectory.

To the south of Chester one side of the rectangle of city walls overlooks the River Dee and there is a castle, first built of wood in 1069 and rebuilt in stone by Henry III. Behind the castle in Grosvenor Street is the Grosvenor museum where there is an exibition showing the life and work of a military town such as Chester.

*Chester's galleried streets, known as The Rows, vividly evoke medieval times.
Today, many smart shops are sheltered behind the colonnades.*

The whole estuary of the Dee which runs into the Irish Sea
was once busy with shipping. Chester was an important port but
silting and the decay of the shipping business has taken its toll and
today the Dee is an area of shallow channels and sandbanks over
which the tide moves with dramatic speed.

The view across to North Wales remains spectacular, with
the Snowdon range rising in craggy splendour against the sky.
This was the view that inspired Turner and is particularly
memorable at sunset when the orange tints of the sky contrast with
the purple-blue mountains of Snowdonia.

At the sea end of the estuary is Hilbre island, which can be
walked to at low tide and where seabirds and waders gather in large
numbers. Permission to visit must be obtained from the Depart-
ment of Leisure Services and Tourism, and a sharp eye needs to be
kept on the tide which sweeps in swiftly to surround the island.

The sandy southern and western shores of the Wirral peninsula lend themselves to leisure pursuits, beach resorts and golf
courses. On the north side, however, there is a built-up area, an
extension of Liverpool which lines the bank on the north side of the
Mersey.

WILD MOUNTAINS AND GREEN VALLEYS

The traveller entering Wales from the green valleys of the Severn is soon aware of a change. Not only do the road signs direct you to places with unpronounceable names, but the landscape itself seems to acquire a different identity. Instead of green meadows, there are small fields, stubbornly holding their own against the scrubland overlooking them from the valley watersheds. There are moorlands – on good days rising gloriously into blue skies, but at other times sombre with mists. Human inhabitants are different too. The stone and flint buildings in the small villages huddle together for protection against the elements, and castles, now gaunt and ruined, rise up on the hills and crags.

There is a feeling of antiquity about Wales, a feeling of the continuity of life; the Cambrian Mountains are among the oldest in Britain and the lonely shepherd on the Denbigh Moors, the fishermen off the Pembroke shore and the slate workers at Blaenau Ffestiniog all represent traditional ways of life that have existed since before the Roman occupation. Wales has undergone many changes since Roman times and has been invaded by Anglo-Saxons, Normans and the English. However, the country has strong roots that have remained firmly in the Celtic earth. From these Celtic roots springs the imaginative and lyrical quality of Welsh life, embodied in such men as Lloyd George, Dylan Thomas and Vaughan Williams. It is this magical quality that makes Wales a rewarding land for travellers. A land of moods and contradictions, and of memorable occasions, whether it is a thunderstorm on Snowdon or a cloudless day in the Brecon Beacons; a Welsh lamb hot pot in a country hotel or laver bread at a village café.

There is a huge variety of scenery in this mountainous country. In the south, the bare grassy slopes of the Brecon Beacons make a sharp contrast to the mining valleys of Glamorgan. The farmlands of Dyfed are an appropriate foil to the rugged coastal cliffs along the south-west coast. Central Wales is a land of hidden lakes and reservoirs which are not always easy to get to. The walker or trail-rider, by leaving the highways, obtains a vision of Wales that is long remembered. This land of Powys is the least

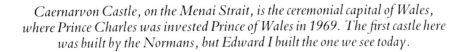

Caernarvon Castle, on the Menai Strait, is the ceremonial capital of Wales, where Prince Charles was invested Prince of Wales in 1969. The first castle here was built by the Normans, but Edward I built the one we see today.

inhabited part of the country and possesses wooded hills, lakes, waterfalls, fast-flowing streams and a large population of animals and birds, some of them rare. To the north is Snowdonia National Park, a wonderland of mountains and valleys, ranging from the slatey austerity of the Llanberis Pass to the wooded intimacy of Betws-y-Coed and the Vale of Conway.

Wherever you go in Wales the feeling of history is strong. When the Normans arrived here, they tried to subdue the country by allowing their powerful barons to take over as much land as they could control from the massive castles they erected. The English, under Edward I, attempted to dominate the Welsh, and in particular the Glendowers, a father and son who fought fiercely for the independence of the country. Eventually, in Tudor times, peace was restored and Henry VII, a descendant of both the Glendower family and the Plantagenets of England, was supported by the Welsh in the Wars of the Roses. It was not until 1536, however, during the reign of Henry VIII, that Wales was joined to England by the Statute of Union.

South and Central Wales

The county of Gwent, to the west of the River Wye, was once an embattled region where great castles were built in the hilly countryside. To the west of Monmouth lies Raglan Castle – a fifteenth-century fortress which saw action in the Wars of the Roses. Later Gwent, like the rest of Wales, was inhabited by Royalist supporters and was under siege by Cromwell's troops for ten weeks before surrendering. Lord Raglan, a descendant of the original owners of the castle, was in command of the British troops during the Crimean War. He lived at Cefntilla Court, between Raglan Castle and Usk, and his home contains many relics of the Crimea.

The three castles which controlled the routes in and out of south Wales stand north-west of Monmouth. One of these is at Skenfrith, a pretty village on the Monnow River surrounded by green hills. Also on the Monnow is the Norman castle of

Grosmont, and its little village set on a slope above the river. The third castle is White Castle, on the road from Skenfrith to Abergavenny. Abergavenny, an attractive town set amid high green hills, is the entrance to the Brecon Beacons National Park. The ruined castle to the south-west of the town was built by a Norman baron, Hameline de Balun, in the eleventh century. In the twelfth century it was the scene of a massacre of Welsh lords by William de Braose.

From Abergavenny, two roads skirt the Brecon Beacons. The road to the south passes the upper part of the Glamorgan and Gwent mining valleys. The other road runs north-west along the Usk Valley, between the Beacons and the Black Mountains. The scenery of the Beacons is varied, with forests and moors; and downland slopes, which are excellent for walking, offering superb views towards England over the Black Mountains, and to the Bristol Channel and Exmoor.

On the Usk route to Brecon is Crickhowell, a small, pleasant town with Georgian houses and a ruined castle. From the town a road leads to the Agen Allwed cave, a two-and-a-half-mile cavern. Two miles from Crickhowell, along the main road, is Tretower Court, a medieval manor house in an exceptionally good state of preservation; and Tretower Castle, a twelfth-century fortress designed to prevent Welsh raids down the Usk Valley (but which was not strong enough to prevent Owen Glendower from destroying it in 1403).

If you take the A465, which goes through Abergavenny and to the south of the Brecon Beacons, you will eventually meet the A49. This is the continuation of the M4 motorway, which crosses

The famous Rhondda valley is much built-over along its river, but above there is wild moorland and close by are the Brecon Beacons.

the Severn Bridge and continues along the coast at Swansea. Along the way, the M4 passes the capital of Wales, Cardiff, a busy seaport on the Bristol Channel.

Although its history goes back to the time of the Romans, Cardiff is predominantly a product of the Industrial Revolution, at which time its population grew from 1,000 to over 200,000 in less than a century. At the centre of the city, in Cathays Park, is the spacious Civic Centre built in the early twentieth century beside the River Taff. South of the park is Cardiff Castle, erected on the site of the Roman camp. The medieval castle was begun in 1093 with the original stone building of Robert of Gloucester, son of Henry I. This was added to and adapted in subsequent centuries and during the Tudor and Stuart periods the castle became more of a manor house than a fortress. Also to the south of the City Centre

Below: The Brecon Beacons National Park is a region of great beauty with steep grassy slopes, cliffs, moorlands and gorges through which tumble mountain streams.

is Cardiff Arms Park, home of Welsh rugby. Two and a half miles to the north is Llandaff Cathedral, founded in the sixth century and rebuilt in stone by the Normans in the twelfth century.

The Cardiff docksides, though no longer as busy as they were when coal was king, still see a good deal of coming and going. To the west of the old coaling port of Barry the grimy world of coal has been replaced by beach resorts and country parks. Along the west-facing coast around Porthcawl there are several sandy beaches; and beyond the iron foundries of Port Talbot is Swansea and the Gower Peninsula.

Oxwich Bay lies on the south coast of the Gower Peninsula and is surrounded by dunes and a verdant countryside which is a national nature reserve.

This secluded peninsula, projecting into the Bristol Channel, is a lovely surprise after a journey through the predominantly industrial coast of south Wales. Green slopes, narrow winding lanes, small farms, rocky cliffs and sheltered coves combine to make a pretty landscape by the sea. The nearest resort to Swansea is The Mumbles, an engaging rendezvous for Swansea people, who keep their small sailing crafts along the promenade where the world's first tram railway ran. From The Mumbles a road runs westwards, aross the peninsula, to Worms Head. This is a sharp, spiny ridge and its name comes from the Old English word for sea monster. There is a splendid view of the sands along Rhossili Bay from Worms Head, and you can see across Carmarthen Bay to the estuary of the Taf and Twyi rivers. Laugharne, home of the poet Dylan Thomas, is situated on the estuary, and this is where Thomas wrote most of his play, *Under Milk Wood*.

To the west of Laugharne is the enchanting seaport of Tenby, with its picture-postcard harbour, round which stand pastel-coloured Georgian houses. A castle was erected on the Tenby promontory in the twelfth century and many of the town's most ancient houses are situated within the castle walls. Tenby's five beaches make it a popular resort in the summer and visitors can

A beach stretches to the small harbour of the walled town of Tenby, which has a
fifteenth-century Merchant's House and the thirteenth-century Church of St.
Mary. Caldy Island, with its Cistercian abbey, is a boat trip away from Tenby.

also cross to Caldy Island, inhabited by Benedictine monks who
make chocolates and perfumes which are on sale to the public.

On the northern arm of the Pembroke Peninsula is St.
David's Cathedral, set in a green hollow by the sea. An earlier
church on this site was destroyed by Norse invaders. St. David's
was founded in the twelfth century by Bishop Peter de Leia, and
was added to up until the seventeenth century. It is the Cathedral of
the Patron Saint of Wales and the shrine of St. David has been a
place of pilgrimage for centuries. St. David's also houses the tomb
of Edmund Tudor, father of Henry VII. Though small, the
cathedral is impressive and the spiritual atmosphere that surrounds
it is enhanced by its secluded setting beside the sea.

From St. David's Head the coast turns eastwards as it begins
its journey to north Wales along Cardigan Bay. This is a very fine
section of the coastal footpath which runs all the way along the
Pembroke Peninsula. Here the path winds along the edge of preci-
pitous cliffs, against which the Atlantic breakers crash, making a
spectacular frothy display. It then takes you past Strumble Head,
an important landmark in the days of sail and steam and still used
by pilots as a reference point on the route across the Atlantic.

The stretch of coast to the east of Strumble Head, leading round to Fishguard, is where England was last invaded by a foreign power. A French force landed here in 1797, during the Napoleonic Wars. A meeting between the English and the French took place at the Royal Oak Inn, and the French were persuaded to give up their hopeless venture. The Inn still survives, and relics of this strange occasion are preserved there. Fishguard was the setting for Dylan Thomas's *Under Milk Wood*, and inland from the town is Mynydd Prese, a 536 m (1,768 ft) hill from which the blue stones of Stonehenge were quarried. From Fishguard the coast continues northwards, past the university town of Aberystwyth.

Aberystwyth lies in central Wales; a remarkably empty part of the country where, apart from the activities of foresters and farmers, nature has remained untouched. In the heart of this region are the spas of Builth Wells and Llandrindod Wells. Both fashionable places at which to take the waters in the eighteenth and nineteenth centuries, they are now centres for open-air holidays. Llandrindod Wells, where the waters can still be taken lies on the River Ithon. This is a tributary of the River Wye, which passes through Builth Wells. Near to Llandrindod Wells is the Roman fort of Castell Collen; relics from here can be seen at the Llandrindod Wells Museum. The surrounding countryside is hilly and wooded – ideal for walking, riding and fishing.

To the north of the Wells is Rhayader, a small, rural town. From here you can visit the Elan Valley and Claerwen Reservoirs, four narrow lakes among wooded hills. To the east are the strange, dome-like hills of the Radnor Forest. Radnor was once a hunting area, hence the name 'forest' which did not necessarily denote a wooded region.

The road from Aberystwyth to the border town of Welshpool cuts across the centre of Wales. Slightly to the north of the road lies Plynlimon, the source of the rivers Severn and Wye. The 748 m (2,468 ft) high hills are notorious for their wet, boggy slopes, from which the rivers start their journey to the sea. From the heights of Plynlimon you can enjoy splendid views across central Wales and north-west, to Cader Idris, the southernmost edge of the Snowdonia National Park.

North Wales

The Snowdonia National Park stretches from the Dovey River to Conway Bay, on the north coast of Wales. The Park contains the most dramatic scenery in Gwynedd and Clwyd – counties which also include Anglesey, the Lleyn Peninsula, the Denbigh Moors and the Clwyd Valley.

At the southern entrance to Snowdonia is the attractive town of Machynlleth, with its many eighteenth-century houses. One of these, the mansion of Plas Machynlleth, was presented to the town by its former owner, Lord Londonderry. The landscape around Machynlleth is striking. To the east the valley of Dovey (Afon Dyfi) climbs towards Dinas Mawddwy. Dinas Mawddwy was once the lair of the Red Robbers of Mawddwy who terrorized the neighbourhood before they were caught and executed in 1554. Straight ahead, to the north, the A487 climbs through the Dyfi Forest towards Cader Idris (887m; 2,927ft). The mountain's steep slopes rise from a green valley and present an impressive spectacle – persuading the onlooker that there could be some truth in the legend that whoever sits at its summit, in the chair of the Giant Idris, will wake up either a poet or a madman.

Beyond Cader Idris is Dolgellau, a village of stone and grey

Left: The Elan Valley Reservoir near Rhayader is in a pretty setting of hills and valleys. It provides water for Birmingham via a 73-mile-long aqueduct.

Below: The hills and valleys around Dolgellau are popular walking country and include the mountain of Cader Idris to the south.

slate, brightened up in summer by a mass of glowing flowers. This is the centre of a superb area for walks. These include the precipice walk on the hills across the Mawddach River, and the walk along the north bank of the Mawddach Estuary to Barmouth (which John Ruskin claimed could only be equalled by the walk from Barmouth to Dolgellau).

From Dolgellau, to the north-east, the land rises rapidly to Lake Bala and Lake Vyrnwy, lying high in the Berwyn Mountains. The waters from these lakes flow eastwards. Lake Bala becomes the River Dee; and the waters of Lake Vyrnwy flow down the River Vyrnwy to join the River Severn. Narrow roads join the lakes; the road at the south-western end of Bala is particularly picturesque and climbs Bwlch-y-Goes, the highest pass in Wales.

The old village of Llanwddyn, on Lake Vyrnwy, was drowned when the reservoir was made between 1880 and 1890. The village of Bala, however, has survived – the earliest remains, a tower in the village, and at the north-east corner of the lake, are

The Italianate village of Portmeirion, built by Sir Williams Clough Ellis, is a delightful folly which brings pleasure to all who visit it.

Snowdon is the highest mountain in England and Wales and, according to Welsh mythology, is the burial place of the giant Rhita Fawr, slain by King Arthur.

Norman. The lake, known in Welsh as Llyn Tegid after Tegid the Bald, a fifth-century chieftain, is a popular place for sailing and sail-boarding; and the wooded countryside around it is ideal for walking and pony-trekking.

Continuing north from Dolgellau the road arrives at Penrhyndeudraeth, in the foothills of Snowdon (1,080 m; 3,560 ft) and at the point where the coast turns westwards along the Lleyn Peninsula, reaching out into the Irish Sea. On a peninsula to the south, a mile away, is the most enchanting folly in all Wales, Portmeirion. This is an Italian village built by the architect William Clough Ellis who, between the 1930s and 1950s, created a village in a pleasant, wooded valley overlooking the estuary. Here you can see an Italian Romanesque church tower, a colonnaded bath house (echoing the architecture of Palladio), cottages, formal gardens and fountains evoking the atmosphere of Italy. This original and entertaining complex is now used as hotel accommodation for visitors.

Two miles further west, over the embankment which crosses the Glaslyn Estuary, is Porthmadog. Formerly a port for the Blaenau Ffestiniog slate quarries, today this attractive little town is a holiday centre. The narrow-gauge train, which once carried slate, now takes passengers up the lovely green valleys to the slate qarries.

From Porthmadog three roads set off to different parts of the north-west corner of Wales. A secondary road runs eastwards to the point of the Lleyn Peninsula, another curves northwards to Caernarvon, while the third sets off to the north, into high Snowdonia, through the village of Beddgelert. This pretty village is much visited, not only for its lovely setting in a wooded valley on the southern slope of Snowdon, but also for the grave of Gelert, the faithful hound of Llewellyn the Great. Llewellyn left his dog in charge of his son and, returning to find it smeared with blood, assumed the dog had killed the child. In anger and dismay Llewellyn slew it but later, when he found a dead wolf and the child alive, the truth dawned on the great Welsh leader, and he made a shrine to his faithful hound.

From Beddgelert the A498 climbs to the lakes of Llyn Dinas and Llyn Gwynant, offering beautiful views of Snowdon across the valley. A road on the left at the top of the climb will take you higher, to Pen-y-Pass and one of the starting points for a walk to the summit of Snowdon. From here the Llanberis Pass, with its rocky screes and forbidding precipices, descends to Llanberis. From here there is another route up and a railway for those who prefer the easy way up: a one-hour trip to the top.

From the road junction at the Pen-y-Gwyd Hotel, the A498 continues to Capel Curig, the famous centre for open air activities – a gathering place for climbers, trekkers, canoeists, bird-

Waterloo Bridge, built to commemorate Wellington's victory over Napoleon in 1815, crosses the Conway River at Betws-y-Coed in a pretty wooded valley.

The view of the north Wales resort of Llandudno, from Great Orme's Head which is reached by a tramway built in 1903, stretches to Little Orme's Head.

watchers, fishermen and all who enjoy taking part in outdoor activities. The scenery is splendid in all directions. To the west, the A5 climbs to solitary Llyn Ogwen, surrounded by the rocky heights of Tryfan and Glydr Fawr. To the east, the road descends through a wooded valley, past the Swallow Falls, to Betws-y-Coed, which lies in the wooded Llugwy Valley at the point where it meets the Conway River.

The Conway Valley, where green hills and tranquil villages are in complete contrast to the rugged landscapes of central Snowdonia, leads northwards to Conway Castle and the town of

The Menai suspension bridge, built by Thomas Telford, was used for stage coach traffic and has been adapted to take the weight of motor traffic.

Conway, on a pretty estuary. Here, the many sailing boats and cruisers are proof that this is an area where holidaymaking and leisure are the reigning activities. Across the river, the Llandudno peninsula confirms this view. Below the sizeable mass of Great Ormes Head, the resort of Llandudno with its sandy beaches stretches eastwards to Little Ormes Head and Colwyn Bay beyond.

West of Conway and its busy town, the road leads to Bangor and the Menai Strait. The Strait is crossed by bridges for road and rail built by Thomas Telford and Robert Stephenson. The rail bridge, a tubular construction, is no longer used, however. It was

Ruined Beaumaris Castle stands on the swampy edges of the Menai Strait. It was built by Edward I after Prince Magod had sacked Caernarvon.

damaged by fire and has been replaced by a modern, conventional bridge. The Menai bridges lead to Anglesey, a low-lying island which has many interesting relics of Iron Age man and a splendid castle at Beaumaris, which looks east across the Strait to Bangor.

The north-east corner of Wales sometimes suffers by comparison with Snowdonia. This is a pity, for it has several interesting areas rich in history and scenery. Along the north coast, the shore is largely devoted to holiday-makers, with resorts and holiday-camps providing accommodation for visitors from Liverpool and the inland cities.

INDUSTRIAL MIGHT
—— AND ——
HEAVENLY LAKES

The north-west corner of England stretches from the busy industrial area between Manchester and Liverpool, through the plain of Lancaster and the mountains of the Lake District, to the flat lands around the Solway Firth. It is a fascinating region with a varied landscape and many places of historical interest.

In Roman times the northernmost part of this region was in constant danger from the Scots who, having forced the Romans to retreat from the frontier on the River Tay, continued to attack them on the Solway Firth. In Hadrian's time, Governor Aulus Platorius Nepos built a wall (Hadrian's Wall) stretching from the Solway Firth to today's Newcastle-upon-Tyne. However, even this failed to contain the marauding Scots and eventually, when the need for troops became very urgent in Rome, the Romans departed.

The north-west then became the victim of Viking raids, forcing the terrorized inhabitants to move elsewhere. The invaders did not settle in this part of Britain during the Dark Ages, and life did not return to the north-west until the arrival of William the Conqueror. William's rule produced a more stable society and encouraged a return to the land. But the north-west's troubles did not end here – for now feudal lords on both sides of the border kept up incessant warfare. The battles continued until Tudor times when, at long last, the north returned to the peace and quiet of rural life which had unfortunately disappeared with the Romans.

The Industrial Revolution produced dramatic changes to the south of the region, making Liverpool Britain's greatest port and the area around Manchester a busy industrial centre, producing machines and textiles for the rapidly expanding empire. In contrast, in the middle of north-west England lie the Cumbrian mountains, an area that has remained virtually untouched throughout history as it is too wild and unproductive to be useful. Known as the Lake District, it now provides a marvellous natural playground for many of the people who live in and around the industrial cities.

These elaborate gates are the entrance to the park at Warrington, an industrial town on the Mersey. Warrington was the home of Primitive Methodism in the nineteenth century and Joseph Priestley and Malthus were pupils at its Academy.

Manchester's neo-Gothic Town Hall was built by Alfred Waterhouse between
1867 and 1876 and possesses a fine Great Hall with a hammerbeam roof.

Around Industrial Manchester

The Manchester ship canal was built between 1887 and 1894, and
after its completion the city of Manchester and its satellites began
to grow in earnest. Now there was no need to send goods to
Liverpool; they could be shipped from their place of origin,
leading to increased activity in the building of factories and offices
that were linked to the export business. The Manchester area
expanded, its tentacles reaching out to Ashton-under-Lyme,
Oldham, Stockport, Stretford, Salford, and dozens of other
surrounding towns. The urban spread absorbed many of the
former estates of the landed gentry. Sometimes, however, the
newly rich industrialists helped to preserve them, or even built
new mansions in the prevailing neo-Gothic style.

On the face of it, this strange mixture of industrial development and rural preservation does not appear to hold much interest
for the visitor; but, as a cross-section of life in England over the last
300 years, it has its fascination. Manchester itself was, until
recently, the grimiest city in England. Now, with the introduction
of the Clean Air Act and the rebuilding of areas demolished by

German bombers in the Second World War, it is improving rapidly and attracts visitors to its unsuspected features of interest. The cathedral, for instance, dates back to the fifteenth century and originally had chantries for, among others, Henry V. The choir stalls are sixteenth century and so is much of the screen woodwork in the chapels. Near the church is the Cheetham Hospital, founded in the 1700s as a school for poor children, now a Music School. To the south of the centre is Victorian Manchester. There is a fine neo-Gothic Town Hall, the Free Trade Hall – home of the Hallé Orchestra – and also the library and theatre.

There are many fine old buildings in the environs of Manchester. At Prestwich is Heaton Hall, designed by James Wyatt in the eighteenth century. It has a splendidly furnished interior, with pieces from the seventeenth and eighteenth centuries. At Bolton you will find Hall i' th' Wood, a half-timbered house in which Samuel Crompton, inventor of the Spinning Jenny, lived, as well as Smith Hall, a handsome manor house. Chorley is the birthplace of Henry Tate, whose generosity allowed the creation of the Tate Gallery in London. Also at Chorley is Astley Hall, an Elizabethan house furnished with the furniture of Cromwell's time. Near Burnley is Gawthorpe Hall, a Jacobean house and Towneley Hall, a rebuilt medieval mansion.

Liverpool, on the River Mersey, though not a tourist centre, also has many points of interest. It has two cathedrals – the Catholic cathedral, a modern building by Frederick Gibberd, and the Protestant cathedral designed, in the neo-Gothic style, by Sir Giles Gilbert Scott. The centre of Liverpool lies between Pierhead

Liverpool, one of the most important ports in England, grew rich on the sugar, tobacco, rum and slave trade after the first docks were built in 1715.

and St. George's Hall. The Pierhead is flanked by the massive Royal Liver Building, the Cunard Buildings and the Dock Board Offices. Nearby is the Town Hall; designed by John Wood the Elder, it was added to by James Wyatt in the late eighteenth century. Near Lime Street Station is the Walker Art Gallery which houses an excellent collection of Italian, French and German paintings, as well as an oustanding number of British paintings from Tudor to modern times.

Below: Blackpool is the most popular resort in the north-west of England, its famous Illuminations attracting visitors to the town well into the autumn.

The coast of south Lancashire shows little sign of the industrial area inland. Instead, it is devoted to the pursuit of leisure, with resorts such as Southport, Lytham St. Anne's and Blackpool; each catering for a particular clientele. Blackpool is the great popular resort of Lancashire and its famous tower, once accompanied by a giant ferris wheel, is the centre of the entertainment area. There are concert halls, theatres, skating rinks; all the fun of the fair is available to the millions who escape from the industrial cities to the seaside throughout the summer. The season ends with a display of lights, lasting from September to October, known universally as the Blackpool Illuminations.

There are more seaside resorts further north along the coast at Morecambe, near Lancaster. Lancaster is an ancient town, once a Roman camp. On its site the Normans built a castle, which you can still see, overlooking the River Lune on the west side of town. As you follow the coast north of Lancaster, it curves and twists in and out of estuaries, past resorts like Grange-over-Sands, and on to the shipbuilding port of Barrow in Furness, off which lies the gondola-shaped island of Walney. This is the southern shore of Cumbria and to the north lies the magical land of the lakes.

The Lake District

At the centre of the Lake District is a range of bare mountains of volcanic origin, from which lakes stretch outwards like the spokes of a wheel. The most southerly of these lakes are Windermere and Coniston Water. The usual approach to the lakes is through the valley of the Kent River, surrounded by smooth green hills, to Kendal.

At the lower end of the valley, near Levens, is Levens Hall. The largest Elizabethan mansion in England, it is set in a formal garden with much well-maintained topiary work. The garden is surrounded by parkland, in which stands a pele tower of the kind that are common along the borders, designed as they were as a protection against Scottish raiders. Further up the valley, on the west side, is Sizbergh Castle. This small but formidable building is surrounded by beautifully maintained grounds with a fine rock garden.

Kendal is an attractive town and a fitting gateway to the Lake District. Its long Highgate Street runs from the Abbott Hall Art Gallery, housed in an eighteenth-century mansion, to Strickland-gate, named after the family that owns Sizbergh Castle. Kendal has its own castle, built by the Normans, which was the birthplace of Catharine Parr, Henry VIII's last wife.

A road runs westwards from Kendal to Windermere Town and Bowness, that part of the town actually on the lakeside. Bowness is a busy place and, with its numerous hotels and harbour full of steamers, it is very different to the rest of the Lake District.

From Bowness a ferry takes cars and passengers across the lake, over to the western shore, where a road leads up to Sawrey. This is the village where Beatrix Potter – creator of such unforgettable characters as Peter Rabbit, Jemima Puddleduck and Jeremy Fisher – lived. Miss Potter's farm contains many of her

---

Left: Douglas, the capital of the Isle of Man, is set in a wide bay surrounded by hills and has a broad two-mile front lined with Victorian houses.

Above: Levens Hall is a fine old Elizabethan house built round a medieval pele tower and is famous for the topiary work in its garden.

Top right: Ambleside is an attractive little town by the River Rothay, which empties into Lake Windermere, and is a popular centre from which to explore Rydal Water and Grasmere.

drawings, as well as the furniture and utensils that appear in them. This enchanting place is cared for by the National Trust, who say that it is visited by more people than any of their other properties. You can enjoy beautiful walks through the woods above Windermere and along the neighbouring Esthwaite Water, which lies on the road to Coniston.

Coniston Water is a pretty lake with wooded slopes and a pleasant town. On its eastern shore you can visit the house of Brantwood where John Ruskin lived, today a museum to his memory. (There is another Ruskin Museum in Coniston itself.) The most appealing aspect of this lake, however, is the countryside that surrounds it. There is the rocky summit of Coniston Old Man, the wooded heights of Tarn Hows and the delightful village of Hawkeshead with its narrow streets, overhanging buildings and old country pubs. North of Coniston and Windermere, over a ridge of hills from which there are fine views, is Ambleside – a town well-suited as a centre for the exploration of the most enchanting parts of the Lake District.

From Ambleside it is only a short distance to Rydal Water and Grasmere. Wordsworth owned properties in these two villages and both his cottage and his house are open to the public. He first lived at Grasmere in the small Dove Cottage and later acquired Rydal Mount, a grander house, overlooking Rydal Water. Here he received many visitors, all anxious to meet him, whom he came to regard as a nuisance. Rydal Water is a small lake surrounded by steep tree-and-bracken-covered slopes, connected to Grasmere by a fast-flowing stream which runs through the Rydal Woods. From above the woods, at Loughrigg Terrace, there is a magnificent view of Grasmere, and its village, which is situated on flat ground which rises rapidly to the bare slopes of Helm Crag.

Bottom: Coniston Water – overlooked by the mountain, the Old Man of Coniston – is the lake on which Donald Campbell was killed while trying for a new world water speed record in 1967.

An alternative road from Ambleside, passing to the south of Loughrigg, will take you to the Langdale Valley, where there is a splendid view of the Langdale Pikes – a popular and not too difficult climb – and on to routes leading up to the higher summits of Sca Fell and Great Gable.

From Grasmere, the A591 continues north to Thirlmere, passing Helvellyn (which can be climbed from Wythburn and Thirlspot). At the northern end of Thirlmere is Castle Rock and a road leading to St. John's Vale; the main road takes you on to Keswick, at the head of Derwentwater. Keswick is a small town and in its centre is a distinctive timbered Moot Hall, round which a market operates. The house at the end of the town square is Greta Hall, the home of Robert Southey. From Keswick a road running on the east shore of the lakes, along wooded banks, leads to the

Below: Derwent Water is a beautiful lake with wooded islands and the town of Keswick lying to the north of the lake-side landing stages.

Above: Stonethwaite Beck runs into Borrowdale, a delightful Lakeland region of steep hills, crags and wooded valleys.

Left: Steep, stony hills rise to each side of Seathwaite, on the way to such Lakeland summits as Sca Fell and Great Gable.

Jaws of Borrowdale – a narrow valley with steep sides, in which sits a formidable crag called Castle Rock. At the entrance to the valley is the village of Grange, an attractive centre from which to explore the Borrowdale area. From here you can walk over the fells to Watendlath, the setting of *Judith Paris*, one of Hugh Walpole's novels about the Herries family.

The scenery around Borrowdale is superb and becomes more dramatic towards the Stye Head Pass and Great Gable. At the entrance to the Seathwaite Valley is Seatoller and the beginning of the Honister Pass. Here the mountain climbs steeply upwards

Honister Crag looms impressively over Honister Pass, which leads from Borrowdale to the charming lakes of Buttermere and Crummock Water.

before descending to Buttermere and Crummock Water, two relatively little-visited lakes lying either side of the charming village of Buttermere. From Buttermere you can visit Lake Ennerdale, which is surrounded by trees planted by the Forestry Commission and, by continuing round the coastal plain road, you will arrive at the only motor road entrance to Wast Water. This is the most spectacular of all the lakes with its great screes and its phalanx of mountains, which include Sca Fell, Lingmell and Great Gable.

At the north-east corner of the Lake District are the lakes of Ullswater and Hawes Water. Hawes Water is, in fact, a reservoir which, though it lacks much of the shoreline interest of other lakes,

Wasdale, above Wast Water, is one of the wildest Lakeland Valleys, with sheer rock faces and narrow tracks challenging climbers and walkers.

has some fine hills around it. At its southern end you can walk along the Roman road, High Street.

The best approach to Ullswater is from Ambleside, up The Struggle. This narrow, winding lane was given its name in the days of the horse and cart, and shouldn't present too much difficulty to a motor car. The Struggle leads to Troutbeck, a long, straggling village of stone houses on the slopes of the Troutbeck Valley. From here, the road joins the main road from Windermere and ascends the Kirkstone Pass; the highest in the Lake District and often impassable when snow falls. On the far side of the Pass is Brothers Water, and then the lovely valley of Patterdale with its surrounding peaks.

Patterdale is a popular centre for walks to Helvellyn, along the Grisedale Valley, bordered by the steep sides of St. Sunday's Crag and Bleaberry Crag. The village of Patterdale is the embarcation point for steamers which take visitors around the lake and across to Howtown, on the south bank. Howtown is a sailing centre and a good starting place for walks along High Street. The road along the lake from Patterdale follows the north bank, passing the path to the pretty waterfall of Aira Force. The path also passes Gowbarrow Park, where Wordsworth saw the daffodils, on its way to Pooley Bridge at the north-east end of the lake.

Here, as often happens on the fringes of the Lake District, the hills suddenly disappear and you find yourself in a green countryside of fields and gentle slopes. On the left is Dalemain, a handsome Georgian house with a fine open park; and Dacre Village. In the centre of the village is the keep of Dacre Castle, named after a Crusader knight who was at the siege of Acre. The River Eamont runs along the centre of this wide, gentle valley, flowing from Ullswater to Penrith and, eventually, joining the River Eden, the tributaries of which flow from the lakeland fells and from the Pennines.

The Eden Valley

The River Eden rises in the Pennines near Kirkby Stephen and flows through Appleby-in-Westmoreland. Appleby is a handsome village with Georgian houses and a castle, the keep of which dominates the main street of Boroughgate. In the seventeenth century the castle was restored by Lady Anne Clifford, an opponent of Cromwell. She also built the St. Anne's Hospital and rebuilt the church of St. Lawrence, where she is buried. The great event of the year at Appleby is the horse fair, held in June, which attracts a colourful crowd of horse traders, gipsies and visitors.

As the River Eden flows north it is joined by the River Eamont, after it has passed Penrith. Penrith is a small, bright town with white painted stone houses, on the east of the M6 motorway to Carlisle. In the town centre are the remains of the castle and, above the town, is the Penrith Beacon – a sandstone tower. From the top you can see Ullswater, and even Scotland, when the weather is fine. Around Penrith there are a number of interesting prehistoric ditches and stone circles.

To the south, on the River Lowther, is the beautiful Lowther Estate – home of the Earls of Lonsdale until 1936. The castle, which looks very impressive from the outside, is actually a shell. However, this does not detract from the decorative sight it presents, in its setting of green parkland. The River Lowther runs through the estate in a deep, wooded valley. Up the steep sides of the valley is the elegant village of Askham, with its sloping main street, bordered by lawns, leading up to rows of cottages.

On its way to the Solway Firth, the River Eden passes another attractive village – Kirkoswald. The ruined castle here was once the home of the Featherstonehaugh family, supporters of Charles I. South of Kirkoswald is a stone circle of 64 stones, 27 of which still stand. They are known as Long Meg and her daughters.

Near Carlisle, the River Eden passes by Corby Castle, more a manor than a fortress, though it was built round a pele tower in the seventeenth century. On the ramparts you can see stone lions, the heraldic emblem of the Howard family, who have owned the estate since 1611.

Carlisle lies to the south of the Roman Wall, between the rivers Caldew and Eden, and was an important military centre during the early years of Roman occupation. Carlisle Castle was built by William Rufus to protect the town from the Scots, who took and lost it several times before Carlisle finally fell to the Duke of Cumberland in 1745. To the south, along Castle Street, is the cathedral, a red sandstone building originally built by the Normans. It was, however, destroyed by the Scots, so that today only two bays in the nave remain from Norman times. Its finest features are the east window and the choir stalls. Also worthy of note is the fact that Sir Walter Scott was married here.

At the southern end of Carlisle, by the railway station, is another castle. It was built by Henry VIII as a defence against the Scots; later to be remodelled by Thomas Telford and Smirke, who designed the dominant drum towers used today as the County Buildings and the County Court.

To the north of Carlisle are fragments of the Roman Wall, though the section between Brampton and Solway Firth is intermittent and lacking in the interest of the central sections. North of the wall is the flat valley of the River Esk, on which lies the town of Netherby. It was to Netherby that young Lochinvar galloped to carry off his bride, in the best traditions of this romantic border between England and Scotland as recounted by Sir Walter Scott in his Border Ballads.

The Eden river flows through wooded banks at Appleby, a charming town with a Norman keep and the centre of a famous annual horse fair.

WOOL, STEEL
— AND —
UNSPOILT
COUNTRY

From the Humber to the borders of Scotland lies one of the most unusual regions of England; combining a vast, green river plain where agriculture has flourished for centuries, the wild, treeless Pennines carved by rivers that have created pastoral dales, and the hill country of Durham and Northumberland, whose rivers, running parallel from west to east, empty into the North Sea.

In the very early days of English history this region was the powerful kingdom of Northumbria, which stretched as far as the Firth of Forth. Northumbria fell to the Danes who arrived in their longships to loot, pillage and, finally, settle on the land. It was during this violent period that the monks who had established Christianity in the region saw their monasteries destroyed. They kept the flame of civilization alive, however, by saving books and treasures even when their monasteries were razed to the ground.

The Norman Conquest brought more harrassment to the north-east, but law and order were gradually restored. Temporal lords built castles to protect their feudal lands and religious leaders erected abbeys, from which they administered the estates where farming and the wool trade began to revive. Throughout the Middle Ages and into the eighteenth century the north-east flourished, its economy based on farming and wool, much of which was exported to the great European wool centres. The nineteenth century brought a dramatic change. The combined resources of coal, iron and wool created great new industries around Tyneside and in southern Yorkshire. Towns began to spread uncontrollably as agricultural workers left the land to take up work in the factories.

The rich and tumultuous history of the north-east, which includes centuries of border warfare with the Scots, has left a fascinating and varied landscape for the visitor to explore. Castles, abbeys and manor houses abound, as do lonely hilltop farms and stone-built villages. There are seaside resorts and compact fishing ports along the coast, and large elegant cities and busy industrial towns along the valleys and plains. Above all there is the natural beauty of mountain, moor, valley and sea; as characteristic of the

Swaledale, which runs into the Vale of York near Richmond, is a deep and beautiful dale in which are the ruins of two priories.

north-east as the people themselves – a hospitable, down-to-earth lot, whose dry sense of humour is as heartwarming as the quality and abundance of their food.

The Vale of York

The flat land of the Vale of York stretches from the River Tees in the north across the Humber into south Yorkshire, where the green farmlands disappear into a densely populated industrial area. The manufacturing towns stretch from Sheffield, a big steel centre, to Leeds, where traditional textile-manufacturing skills have made the city a world centre for the ready-to-wear clothing industry. Surprisingly, the countryside has not been completely overwhelmed by the urban sprawl, nor have all the great architectural wonders of the past been engulfed.

Sheffield is particularly fortunate, being tucked into the east slopes of the High Peaks. Even to the east, where the industrial cities of Rotherham and Doncaster lie along the River Don, there are patches of open countryside and the ruins of castles surrounded by grassy slopes and trees are to be found at Conisbrough and at Tickhill – to the north is the ruin of Pontefract Castle, where Richard II was murdered.

Pontefract is at the eastern end of the string of industrial towns with famous names such as Halifax, Bradford, Huddersfield, Wakefield and Leeds. To the north is the rural Vale of York. To the east, on the River Ouse, is Selby. This Georgian town is renowned for its abbey church, which stands imposingly in the

Halifax was created by the cloth trade and possesses a fine Piece Hall where the cloth market operated. The Town Hall was designed by Sir Charles Barry.

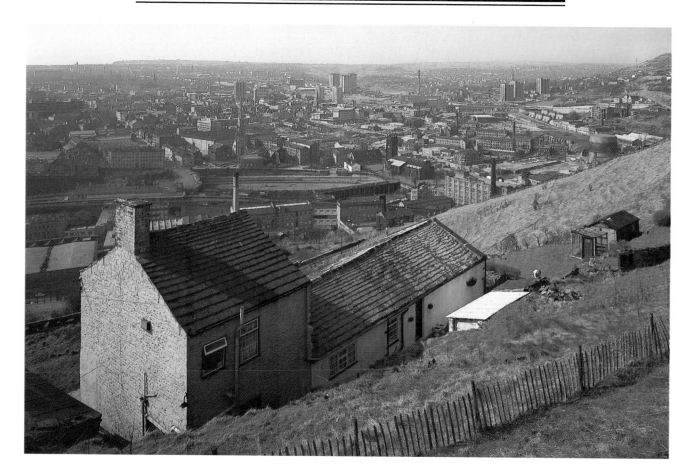

main street, still intact due to refurbishment after the destructive period of the Dissolution. Selby Abbey was founded in the eleventh century by Benedictine monks and has much splendid Norman and Early English architectural features, including the Decorated Period choir and the fine east window.

To the north of Selby, also on the River Ouse, is the city of York, with its medieval city walls and magnificent cathedral. York was a Roman city and traces of the fort still survive at the Multangular tower, near Museum Street and the Yorkshire Museum. The centre of the old town lies to the east, along the River Ouse, and stretches to the point where the Foss joins the Ouse. The old town is dominated by the castle, originally built by William the Conqueror but later rebuilt by John Carr as the Assize Courts. Alongside stands the Museum; this building, also by John Carr, was once a women's prison. Before the Castle is Clifford's Tower, a stone, quartrefoil-plan building, standing on the mound where William the Conqueror's first wooden keep was erected.

One of the most nostalgic quarters of the town is The Shambles, a muddle of narrow streets evoking an image of the medieval town: today the buildings are maintained as a showplace and contain small shops. Walking from The Shambles to the cathedral along Low Petergate, you can picture medieval York when the Minster was entirely surrounded by small, timbered buildings.

York Minster, the largest of England's medieval churches, is a masterful combination of the architecture from three periods of English history: Early English in the transepts, Decorated in the

The splendour of York Minster with its medieval stained glass dominates the attractive walled city by the River Ouse.

nave, and Late Perpendicular in the choir and towers. The whole has great unity and power, enhanced in the interior by the magnificent stained-glass windows, examples of the development of this art form over a period of 800 years. An interesting feature of the church is the undercroft, which houses a museum containing remains of Roman York discovered in 1967 during the work of strengthening the tower.

Among the many museums and art galleries in York, the National Railway Museum, near the station, must be singled out. It contains the largest collection of railway engines, carriages and ancillary material connected with rail transport in the world. It is appropriately situated, for the greatest railway entrepreneur of the nineteenth century, George Hudson, was born near York and was three times its Lord Mayor. Other notable residents of York include Guy Fawkes, the artists William Etty and John Flaxman, Robinson Crusoe (described by Defoe as 'a man of York') and John Hansom, inventor of the hansom cab. A replica of the cab, riding down a mock-up of a street in York a 100 years ago, can be seen in the Castle Museum.

Perhaps the greatest pleasure that York offers its visitors is a walk round the three-mile-long ramparts surrounding the city. Along the way you can enjoy memorable views of the Minster and the many other handsome buildings the city is fortunate to possess.

In the Vale of York, to the north of the city, there are many other fine buildings. Eight miles north is Beningborough Hall, a Baroque eighteenth-century house, in which are displayed a collection of paintings from the National Portrait Gallery. On the eastern slopes of the Ure Valley is the thirteenth-century Castle Crayke and its village. From Castle Crayke you can look across the plain to the city of York.

The town of Harrogate lies to the west. This fashionable spa of the eighteenth and nineteenth centuries is now a successful conference centre. The glories of the years during which society people gathered at Harrogate, not only to cure their aches and pains but to mingle with others of the 'spa set', still remain and provide an attractive background to the more commercial gatherings of the present day. In the centre of town you will find the Royal Baths and Assembly Rooms, where thousands took sulphur baths and engaged in social intercourse, and the Royal Hall, which has now had a huge exhibition centre added to it. A short distance away, down Crescent Road, is the Royal Pump Room, built over Harrogate's most famous sulphur spring – appropriately called the Stinking Spaw – today a museum of local life. Beyond the Pump Room are the Valley Gardens where the Magnesia Well and some 30 others bubble up within an area of approximately 100 square yards. Harrogate is fortunate in having plenty of open spaces. The largest is The Stray, a 200-acre park in which William Slingsby discovered the first of the springs that transformed Harrogate from a small country town into the largest spa in the world.

The idea that these were mineral springs which could be exploited in the way they were on the Continent occurred to Slingsby near Knaresborough, where he came across a spring with water that reminded him of water he had drunk abroad. Today the water from limestone caves still drips at the Dropping Well. Objects hung under the percolating water are gradually petrified by the lime deposited on them. Knaresborough is a pretty town on the River Nidd with many Georgian houses. Its fourteenth-century castle was devastated by Cromwell's men, but still retains

Knaresborough, on the River Nidd, has many eighteenth-century houses, with the keep of John of Gaunt's castle rising above the Castle Gardens.

its twin-towered entrance gate, King's Chamber and dungeons. The most famous inhabitant of Knaresborough was Mother Shipton, a lady much respected for her prophecies in the fifteenth century. Her reputation took a mortal blow, however, in 1981. This was the year, according to her prediction, that the world would come to an end!

To the north of Knaresborough, on the River Ure, is an area of great historical interest due to evidence of occupation by Iron Age people who erected the monoliths known as the Devil's Arrows. These 9 m (30 ft) monoliths remain from what was probably a larger monument, but the reason for their existence is a mystery. In the same area, between Aldborough and Borough-bridge, are the remains of the Roman town of Isurium; some relics from there can be seen in the small, local museum.

The impressive ruins of Fountains Abbey in their woodland setting by the River Skeel evoke a world ruled by monarchs but administered by a powerful church.

To the west, on the River Skeel, which joins the River Ure, lies the enchanting Fountains Abbey; a product of the business flair and artistic sensibility of the church in the Middle Ages. The Abbey was founded by Benedictine monks but later taken over by Cistercians, who developed a business in wool from Pennine sheep. Though ruined during the Dissolution, there is enough left of Fountains Abbey to enable the visitor to reconstruct in the mind's eye the glory of the original building. Outside the west lodge is a well-preserved Jacobean building, Fountains Hall – one of the many fine manor houses in the environs of Ripon, which lies along the River Skeel to the north. Others are Markenfield Hall and Newby Hall, a Queen Anne house, both to the south of the town.

Ripon has a small but interesting cathedral, one of the three earliest centres of Christianity in Yorkshire. Only the crypt survives from the early church established by St. Wilfred in the seventh century; the main church is from the twelfth and thirteenth centuries, with aisles added in the sixteenth century.

The most northern of the Yorkshire tributaries of the River Ouse is the River Swale, above which lies the charming town of Richmond – once the seat of a Grey Friars monastery, only the tower remains today. Owing to its commanding position at the entrance to Swaledale, Richmond was a place of great strategic importance, with its castle standing on the edge of a cliff above the river. The keep, built by the Normans, was erected in the twelfth century and the castle continued to be important until the time of the Tudors. Henry VII inherited the name of Richmond from his father, Edmund Earl of Richmond, and bestowed it on his own palace by the Thames, at present-day Richmond, Surrey.

To the east of Richmond, over a ridge of hills which separate the Vale of York from the Tees Valley, lie the Cleveland Hills and the North York Moors.

The Moors and Wolds

From the plateau of the North York Moors the River Esk flows towards the sea at Whitby; and the tributaries of the Derwent, a river which runs in the Vale of Pickering, flow to the south. This small, secluded area with is steep-sided valleys and stone houses is ideal for the walker and for those who love an unspoilt and tranquil countryside; it also has many places of interest along its borders. To the east, along the edges of the Vale of York, is Helmsley; an attractive market town with a ruined castle at the foot of the Cleveland Hills. To the north is the great Cistercian Abbey of Rievaulx which, like Fountains, became wealthy through the wool trade. Rievaulx represents the highest achievements of monastic architecture in England. Not far away is another Cistercian Abbey, Byland, which was founded in 1147 (a few years after

An eleventh-century castle built by a Norman Earl of Richmond looks out over the town of Richmond and the River Swale which flows into the Vale of York.

The old village of Staithes lies in a narrow ravine leading down to a tiny harbour where fishermen still dry their nets.

Rievaulx). Nearby is the village of Coxwold where Laurence Sterne was a curate. He wrote *A Sentimental Journey* and *Tristram Shandy* in his house here, now called Shandy Hall.

On the east side of the moors the interest lies not in monastic life but in the expansion of leisure activities, which began in the eighteenth century and has developed into a major industry during this century. In the eighteenth century, the leisured classes began to frequent the seaside village of Scarborough for its spa, which possessed not only mineral springs but also salt water wells, whose curative properties were being promoted by Dr. Richard Russell. The health-giving salt water was imbibed with port or milk, and was bathed in; at first in private tubs, but an early engraving of the beach at Scarborough in the 1880s shows naked gentlemen cavorting about the sands! In due course the business of the spa was organized, a spa building set up and bathing carried on from bathing machines at regular scheduled times – with ladies and gentlemen bathing separately.

There could hardly have been a better setting for this new social activity, for Scarborough sits on a ring of cliffs overlooking a sandy bay. On the promenade here the spa still operates, though today it is more of a centre of entertainment than a health estab-lishment. Down by the harbour, overlooked by Scarborough Castle, the scene is much as it was when Anne Brontë was sent to

The colourful little port of Whitby built Captain Cook's Endeavour. Centuries before the divided churches of Britain had accepted Roman authority at Whitby.

stay in Scarborough for her health; fishing boats and pleasure craft jostle for a place along the quayside, and the gulls wheel and shriek overhead as the day's catch is landed. In Anne's day there were no funfairs or amusement arcades, but no doubt the whelk and cockle stalls did as brisk a business as they do today.

The coast from Scarborough to Whitby is most attractive. The Cleveland Hills ring the edge of the North Sea, with cliffs along which lie small sandy resorts like Ravenscar and Robin Hood's Bay. Whitby, at the mouth of the River Esk, is an evocative little fishing port with terraces of houses along the steep banks of the river. Above the port stand the gaunt ruins of Whitby Abbey, which was shelled by the German Fleet in the First World War. The original abbey, destroyed by the Danes, was founded in the seventh century and was the home of Caedmon, the first English poet. A monument to Caedmon stands in the churchyard of St. Mary's, the parish church. It was in Whitby that the *Endeavour* was built; the ship in which Captain James Cook, a resident of the town, sailed around the world. The exploits of this great sea captain are commemorated in a statue which stands on the promenade.

To the south of Scarborough lies a flatter coast of popular resorts with large expanses of sand. Among these are Filey, Bridlington and Hornsea; all with the traditional jovial character of a north-country holiday resort. From Bridlington you can walk out to Flamborough Head, a chalk peninsula with sheer cliffs – an area where sea birds are protected. It was off Flamborough Head that the American captain, Paul Jones, engaged an English ship in 1779 and captured it, although his own ship sank after the engagement.

Inland from this coast are the gently undulating Yorkshire Wolds, a sheep-rearing area which provided much of the wool so important to the economy of the north-east – first to the monasteries and then to the mills of west and south Yorkshire.

The Pennines

At their southern extremity the Pennines are squeezed between vast, industrial areas: Manchester and Bradford on one side, and Leeds on the other. They still manage, none the less, to preserve some of their untrammelled wilderness, though only a few miles from the satanic mills. Near the manufacturing town of Keighley the road rises to the moors made immortal by Charlotte and Emily Brontë. Haworth, with its narrow cobbled streets, was the home of the Brontë family. The stone parsonage they lived in is now a Brontë museum. Both Charlotte and Emily are buried in the village church; and the Black Bull Inn, which was their elder brother Branwell's hideaway, still sells the beer and spirits to which Branwell became addicted and that led to his early death. Despite its proximity to industrial Keighley, and the prevalence of shops and cafés trading off the Brontë connection, Haworth retains much of the grim atmosphere which led three imaginative women to write original and haunting books and their brother to

In this building at Haworth lived the Reverend Patrick Brontë and his family, Charlotte, Emily, Anne and Branwell. The three girls all wrote outstanding novels, but Branwell died an unhappy alcoholic.

drown his disenchantment in drink. To the north of Keighley, across the River Aire, lies the moor made famous in the song *On Ilkley Moor baht'at*.

The Aire Valley is one of the principal corridors of communication across the Pennines, providing access by road, rail and the Leeds-Liverpool canal, which all pass through Skipton. This busy market town was once a strategic strongpoint guarded by the castle of the Clifford family, which stands at the top of the High Street. The parish church contains many Clifford tombs. The family, with the Percys of Northumberland, ruled over the north of England for many generations but, like so many other Royalist families, were overwhelmed by Cromwell.

Upstream from Skipton the Aire travels through a wild and rugged terrain, where bare hills and rocky gorges take the place of the rural countryside characteristic of the lower dales. North of the little village of Malham is Malham Cove, a natural amphitheatre bordered by limestone cliffs. The River Aire springs from Malham

Tarn to the east. To the north-east is Gordale Scar, a rocky chasm with a spectacular double waterfall.

The River Wharfe flows in a parallel valley to the east, passing the ruins of Bolton Abbey. The Wharfedale villages of Kettlewell and Grassington are gathering places for walkers, as they are for the cavers who explore the underground limestone caverns of Great and Little Whernside.

This part of the Pennines is a watershed between several important rivers flowing to the east and west down famous dales; to the west is Ribblesdale, and to the east Wensleydale – home of the cheese. Down the River Ure are Aynsgarth and its waterfall, Aynsgarth Force; four miles away is Bolton Castle. Mary Queen of Scots was imprisoned there after she fled from Scotland in 1568.

To the north, the River Eden begins its long journey to the Solway Firth. Near the source of the Eden, on the slopes of High Seat, the Swale Rivers starts its own journey to the North Sea. Swaledale is the deepest and, in the opinion of some, the most beautiful of the Yorkshire Dales. It plunges through the narrow Kisdon Gorge and is crossed by the Pennine Way at Keld Village. Beyond Swaledale the Pennines pass into Durham and the high ground around Barnard Castle. The castle, whose ruins stand above the little market town, once guarded the routes along the River Tees. It was founded in the twelfth century by Bernard

Below: The River Wharfe, which rises high in the Pennines, flows through Wharfedale, a lovely area of rolling hills popular with walkers.

Right: Britain's finest Norman cathedral, at Durham, stands high on a bluff encircled by the River Weare and contains the tomb of St. Cuthbert of Lindisfarne.

The River Tyne has a busy estuary lined with shipyards and warehouses above which cranes raise their heads over the ships and trawlers that crowd the banks.

Balliol and confiscated in the thirteenth due to the revolt of John Balliol. (John Balliol's father was founder of Balliol College, Oxford in 1263.) One of the most interesting features of the town of Barnard Castle is the Bowes Museum, which contains paintings and exhibits concerned with local history.

To the north-east of Barnard Castle, near Staindrop, is Raby Castle, a fourteenth-century stronghold at which some 700 knights could gather when the castle's lords, the Nevilles, called a meeting. Richard Neville, a fifteenth-century descendant, became Earl of Warwick – famous as the 'Kingmaker' of the Wars of the Roses. The castle, which stands in open parkland occupied by herds of deer, was refurbished in the seventeenth and nineteenth centuries and provides a valuable picture of life in feudal times.

Between Barnard Castle and Hadrian's Wall lies almost empty moorland scored by the valley of the Tees, which flows south, and by the Tyne, which flows north. The Tyne runs from the slopes of Hard Hill to Haltwhistle, about half a mile from Hadrian's Wall. In this area you will find the central and best preserved part of the wall built by Hadrian in an attempt to defend Britain's borders from the marauding Scots. At Chesterholme on the Stangate (a road running parallel to the wall, built by the Romans as a supply line to the troops) ramparts and central buildings of a fort are visible. Housesteads is the best example of the forts which were built every 7 miles along the wall. Remains of its central headquarters, granaries, workshops, stables and barracks stand out above ground. From Housesteads there is an impressive view of the wall running east and west along the undulating terrain; the last rampart of the Empire the Romans were obliged to abandon in 323.

North of the wall is lovely, rolling countryside, stretching over the Northumberland National Park to the Cheviot Hills and the Scottish border beyond. The Forestry Commission has planted trees over the barren moorland and nature trails have been made through the woods, which provide shelter for deer, foxes, squirrels and many different species of wild birds. The largest of the forests is the Kielder Forest, where there is a natural history museum at Lewisburn, by the reservoir in the centre of the forest.

Housesteads was a fort along this part of the Roman wall which the Emperor Hadrian ordered to be built in AD 120 to keep out raiders from the north.

Along the North-east Coast

The north-eastern corner of England, flanked to the west by the Scottish border and to the east by the North Sea, is a fascinating part of Britain, rather neglected by the tourist. Crossed by rivers, the chief of which is the Coquet, rising in the Cheviot Hills, the countryside is rich in history and varied in scenery. Once part of the Kingdom of Northumbria, it later became the private kingdom of the powerful Percy family. Later, Percys played a part in the drawing up of the Magna Carta. For his part in the conquest of Scotland, Richard Percy was rewarded with the wardenship of Bambrugh and Scarborough Castles and the lands of Robert the Bruce in Carrick – the base on which the Percy lands and power grew. The seat of the Percys was at Alnwick on the River Aln; the Percy Castle still stands there. Although it was largely rebuilt during the eighteenth and nineteenth centuries by the Duke of Northumberland, the castle has retained its medieval atmosphere; especially at the gatehouse and barbican, on the parapets of which stone figures create a dramatic effect. The inner ward contains a fourteenth-century gatehouse and dungeons. Inside the castle are reconstructed rooms, including a dining room, library and drawing room, all furnished and displaying a fine picture collection, including a Canaletto of the castle, as seen from the present-day north bank car park.

To the south of Alnwick lies Warkworth Castle, on the River Coquet. This was the birthplace of Harry Hostpur, who died fighting Lancastrian Henry IV at the Battle of Shrewsbury; an event recorded by Shakespeare in the historical drama, *Henry IV (Part I)*. The castle is superbly sited above the medieval town. The River Coquet – a famous salmon river – cuts a deep ravine through Warkworth, in which a fourteenth-century hermitage is carved out of the rock.

Further up the river is Brinkburn Priory, an Augustinian establishment where a fine church can still be seen. From here the road ascends Coquetdale, close to the bank of the river, to the market town of Rothbury, set among moorlands. The road leads on to Castle Harbottle and then to Alwinton, where English and Scottish wardens of the Marches, arbitrators of border disputes, would meet to try to prevent armed conflict.

Amble, at the mouth of the Coquet, is the last northern coastal port of the industrial area of Tyneside; from here the character of the coast changes. Alnmouth, the harbour of the Aln, is a delightful place with sandy beaches and a protected harbour packed with yachts. Craster, further north, is a tiny port full of fishing boats and bordered by small, stone houses. Some of the finest kippers in Britain are smoked at Craster. Beyond the town you can see the gaunt ruin of Dunstanburgh Castle, which can be reached along a clifftop footpath.

Probably the most impressive castle in the north-east is Bambrugh, rising on a magnificent crag above the little village. It is, perhaps, best seen from across the sandy seashore, along which the North Sea waves break and surge towards the reedy land. Bambrugh Castle was rebuilt by the Armstrong family at the turn of the century, but still possesses its twelfth-century Norman keep and curtain walling. Bambrugh's most famous citizen is Grace Darling who, with her father, the lighthouse keeper, rowed out to sea in a storm to save a vessel in distress. Consequently, Grace's deeds have become synonymous with the spirit of heroism and

The massive battlements of Bamburgh Castle on its huge crag rising out of the flat Northumberland coast make an unforgettable sight.

self-sacrifice. She is buried in the village church; the boat she used is in the museum.

Off-shore are the Farne Islands; a bird sanctuary which can only be visited if special permission is obtained from the National Trust. The solitary, low-lying islands were a place of retreat for St. Aidan, the founder of the Holy Island of Lindisfarne, which lies to the north. Though now only the ruins remain of St. Aidan's priory, Holy Island still retains the haunting atmosphere of the early Christian presence. Aidan and his later followers were not simply dreamy mystics, however, and the remains of the Norman Priory reveal a preoccupation with defence – perhaps the result of lessons learned when Aidan and his men were forced to flee the island with all their precious books during the Danish invasions of the ninth century.

Defence was a major concern of the builders of Berwick-on-Tweed, on the borders of Scotland. The ramparts of the town which, after years of changing hands, became English in 1482, are a fine example of the military style of architecture developed in Italy and France. Today the ramparts and towers present the visitor with innumerable, stirring vistas of town, river and sea, evoking images of the days when England and Scotland were not a United Kingdom but two separate and enemy countries.

THE LAND
— OF —
ROBBIE BURNS

The story of Scotland goes back to the invaders from Ireland who settled on the land inhabited by wild Picts from the north. The first recorded history, however, begins with the Romans, who called this unconquered territory Caledonia. After being forced to retreat behind Hadrian's Wall, the Romans finally departed altogether in 323, but their threat to the Scots was soon replaced by that of the tribes of northern Europe – in particular the Norsemen – who arrived to pillage and, sometimes, to settle, especially on the islands off the north-west coast. The Viking menace led the Scots to unite under Kenneth McAlpine in 844 and here the story of the Scottish nation begins.

The unification of the country did not take place at this time, however, for while the southern Scots were trading and mixing with the English, the Highland Scots remained isolated and resentful of the intrusion of outsiders and at the same time were engaging in bitter and destructive clan warfare amongst themselves. The growing interest of England in annexing Scotland brought some semblance of unity once more, under national heroes such as William Wallace and Robert the Bruce, but this precarious unity was destroyed in 1336. Edward III occupied Scotland and, having captured David II, son of Robert the Bruce, installed him as a puppet king. David's nephew, Robert II, then became the first Stewart king of Scotland, a line which lasted until the exile of Mary Queen of Scots and her death in 1567. Mary's son became James I of England and VI of Scotland and was the first of the Stuart kings of England, but the Stuarts' reign came to an end when George I of the House of Hanover ascended the English throne. The Old and Young Pretenders who claimed the throne through James II tried to reverse this situation in 1715 and 1745, but their attempts brought disastrous results to the Highlanders, who became subjects of intense repression. This lasted until the clearances of the land, between 1780 and 1860; a time when the Highlands were depopulated and mass emigration to America, Australia and New Zealand took place.

Following that period, Scotland developed as a divided country with a beautiful, but poverty stricken Highland region

Jedburgh Abbey was founded by Prince David, later King of Scotland, and is today a magnificent ruin with a fine Norman tower dominating Jed Water.

and central and southern regions which grew wealthy during the industrial age and contained Scotland's two finest cities – Glasgow and Edinburgh.

The dramatic history of Scotland lends added interest to this glorious land. Wherever you go you will find castles, strongpoints, manor houses, roads and monuments which have all played their part in Scotland's story.

The Border Country

The part of Scotland along the frontier with England is within the counties of Borders, on the east, and Galloway, on the west. The River Tweed and its tributaries run through Borders, rivers which drain off the Southern Uplands and the Cheviot Hills. This is a peaceful land of green valleys and swift-flowing salmon rivers, where relics of a turbulent past add interest for the visitor. It is the land of Sir Walter Scott and of bandits, called Reivers, who made life hazardous for the inhabitants already plagued by border raiders from England.

The most populated part of this region is the Tweed Valley and, in particular, the central section of the course of the Tweed, where it is joined by the tributaries which provide water for the tweed mills. The valleys of these rivers make corridors of communication between the towns. Jedburgh is one of these. Its main street rises above Jed Water, alongside which stands the ruin of a noble Abbey church, burned down by English troops in 1523. The ruins are still impressive, with the tower and walls which have three tiers of arches; the west front has the moulding of a rose window. Mary Queen of Scots stayed in Jedburgh in 1566 and her house is now a museum.

Jed Water joins the Teviot which runs down to meet the River Tweed at Kelso. An elegantly laid out market town, Kelso has a spacious cobbled square with an eighteenth-century Court House topped by a Curfew Tower in its centre. The Old Pretender was proclaimed King James VIII here and his son, Bonnie Prince Charlie, stayed here after his defeat in 1745. Near the splendid bridge over the River Tweed stand the remains of the Abbey. Only the façade, transepts and tower are still standing, but they are enough to give an impression of what the whole complex of buildings must have looked like. One mile to the west of Kelso, along the river, lie two castles. One of these, Roxburgh Castle, is now no more than a mound of earth and stones; the other, across the river, is a well-maintained eighteenth-century mansion called Floors Castle, the seat of the Duke of Roxburgh. In the fine park at Floors, a tree marks the spot where James II was killed by an exploding cannon. To the north-west of the castle, on a rock by a small loch, is Smailholm Tower. This is a good example of the defensive towers which were built all over the border country, and Smailholm was the setting for Sir Walter Scott's poem *The Eve of St. John*.

Smailholm is roughly on the eastern border of what is often called Scott Country. The centre of Scott Country is Abbotsford, which lies near Melrose on the River Tweed. Sir Walter Scott lived in Abbotsford for the last 20 years of his life. He bought a farm by the river in 1811 and the marjority of his most important books were written here. The house, to which he added new rooms, demolishing most of the old farm, was presented to him by his creditors when he went bankrupt in 1826 after becoming involved

Sir Walter Scott lived at Abbotsford for the last 20 years of his life, the house reflecting his interest in medieval life and architecture.

in an unsuccessful publishing venture. Today Abbotsford is a museum where you can see an armoury, paintings and a number of historical objects collected by the author.

Melrose is a small country town by the Eildon Hills. The hills are an outcrop of volcanic rock, split into three peaks. They were split, it is said, by the Devil, urged on by a local wizard, Thomas the Rhymer. The hills are also said to be the burial place of King Arthur and his knights. The main feature of the town of Melrose is the Abbey, of which about half the original building remains. Monks from Rievaulx founded the original Abbey which suffered considerable destruction from English raiders in the 1400s. Though repaired by Robert the Bruce, it continued to be attacked and, in the sixteenth century, the Abbey was abandoned to become a stone quarry for buildings in the town.

Another ruined Abbey lies downstream – Dryburgh – which was also abandoned in the sixteenth century. However, in the eighteenth century the estate fell into the hands of Sir Walter Scott's family and, with it, the right to be buried in the Abbey. Sir Walter Scott's tomb is in the north transept; also the tomb of Earl Haig, Field Marshall in charge of the British Army in the First World War, who was born in the nearby village of Bemersyde. To the west of Scott Country is the Ettrick Forest and the busy textile-manufacturing town of Hawick, on the Teviot River. Once a strategic strongpoint, Hawick was destroyed by the English in 1570, and all that remains of the medieval castle is a mound in the town centre.

Further west still is the Wauchope Forest, which forms the watershed between the east-flowing and west-flowing rivers of the border country and the upper reach of Liddesdale, which stretches to the Solway Firth. This is a wild moorland area with a sombre beauty, which reaches a high point at lonely Hermitage Castle – a square, stone building which once belonged to Lord Soulis.

Liddel Water joins the River Esk as it approaches the Solway Firth and crosses into England. Along the Scottish border is Gretna Green, famous for its blacksmith-shop marriages which, by Scottish Law, could be performed by declaration before two witnesses. This form of marriage became illegal in 1840 and today Gretna is a small, undistinguished village trading on its dubious past.

The Southern Uplands

From the Mull of Galloway to the Lammermuir Hills is a country-side of vast, rounded hills, whose valleys run south to the Solway Firth and north to the Central Plain of Scotland. Far less visited than the other parts of Scotland, the Southern Uplands (contained largely in the counties of Dumfries, Galloway and Strathclyde) are historically important. It was here that the Scots first landed from Ireland and that the Christian missionaries, led by St. Ninian, erected the first churches. Both Wallace and Bruce were also based in Scotland's south-west and Scotland's most famous poet, Robert Burns, lived on the west coast.

In the far west the land projects into the North Channel between Scotland and Ireland in the curious hammer-head formation of the Rhins of Galloway. In Loch Ryan, the northern bay of the Rhins, is Stranraer – the ferry port for Larne in Northern Ireland. To the south is Luce Bay, a wide expanse of sea along the eastern edge of which runs the Machars Peninsula. This is a land of farms, where sheep and dairy cattle are raised and also where ancient chapels and ruined castles tell the stories of past struggles.

Liddel Water, which runs along the western end of the border between Scotland and England, was once a battleground for raiders.

Glenluce, at the northern end of the bay, is the largest village in the area and possesses the ruins of a twelfth-century Abbey to which an Eildon wizard, Michael Scott, lured the plague and locked it up in a vault. St. Ninian landed on the southern Isle of Whithorn and founded a monastery at the town of Whithorn in AD 397. The cave to which he retired for meditation is on the coast at Port Castle Bay.

Wigtown Bay is ringed with castles. There is a hill fort near Whithorn Island, ruined Cruggleton Castle near Wigtown and, on the east side of the bay, Carsluith and Barholm Castles. Farther east, along the indented coast, is McLellan Castle at Kirkcudbright, a pleasant town with a spacious waterfront and many eighteenth-century houses along its wide streets. Nearby, to the east, is the ruin of Dundrennan Abbey, where Mary Queen of Scots spent some time before departing to her exile and imprisonment in England.

Dumfries is the largest town along the southern edge of the Southern Uplands and is situated on the River Nith, in one of the three lovely valleys which run from the Uplands to the Solway Firth. In the centre of the town is a tolbooth or guildhall called Mid-Steeple, on which in relief is a plan of Dumfries in the time of Robert Burns. The poet died in the town and his grave is in St. Michael's churchyard. His favourite pub, the Globe Inn, preserves the chair in which he liked to sit. The pleasantest part of Dumfries is by the waterfront, where there is a weir, a six-arch footbridge and a museum in the Old Bridge House. To the north of the town is Lincluden Abbbey, founded for Benedictine nuns in the twelfth century.

The estuary of the Nith stretches out into the Solway Firth and has two points of interest. On the right bank is Sweetheart Abbey, founded by Devorguilla Balliol, mother of King John Balliol. Devorguilla was buried in the Abbey with the heart of her dead husband, which she had carried around with her for sixteen years. On the left bank is Caerlaverock Castle, the fortress of the Maxwells, who lost it and won it back several times during its history. The castle is still surrounded by a water-filled moat and has a vast, impressive gateway. Its interior is a surprising contrast to other parts of the ruin, for it is in elegant Renaissance style, but unfortunately was badly damaged by Covenanters who beseiged the castle in 1640. Nearby, along the low-lying shores, is the Caerlaverock National Nature Reserve, providing a haven for a large number of wild fowl.

The coast along the west of the Southern Uplands is associated with Robbie Burns. Burns was born at Alloway, near Ayr, and his thatched cottage is preserved as a museum. There is another museum at the Tam O'Shanter Inn in Ayr High Street. Ayr is a pleasant town with a river harbour running through its centre and an esplanade along the sandy shore. The harbour is crossed by four bridges – one of which is the Auld Brig which Burns wrote about in his poem *The Brigs of Ayr*. The oldest part of the town lies between the harbour and the sea. Little remains from medieval times, though a twelfth-century tower still stands in the church of St. John the Baptist. This church was incorporated into a Cromwellian fort in the seventeenth century, however, compensation was paid to the town and another church, the Auld Kirk, was erected by the harbour.

The land to the south of Ayr is hilly and has a rocky coast along which is Dunure Castle. Now a ruin on the edge of the sea,

Dunure was where the Earl of Cassilis, head of the Kennedy clan that ruled this part of Scotland, roasted the Abbot of Crossraguel Abbey, which lies inland, in order to obtain the deeds of the Abbey lands. Beyond Dunure is the Magic Brae, a section of road along which a car will run uphill without an engine – an effect which some ascribe to an optical illusion and others to magic!

Further south along the coast is Culzean Castle, an imposing building begun by Robert Adam in the eighteenth century. Now a showplace, Culzean has a Park Centre with an auditorium, a model of Culzean's 565-acre park, and a shop. The house is well maintained by the Scottish National Trust and contains many fine rooms, including one presented to General Eisenhower for his use during his lifetime. Still further south is Ardstinchar Castle, which is near Ballantrae, background for *Master of Ballantrae* by Robert Louis Stevenson.

North of Ayr, the flat sandy coast is a holiday playground for the inhabitants of Glasgow's industrial area. It is also a meeting place for international golfers at the world-famous courses near

Robbie Burns' Greek-style memorial in Alloway near Ayr is surrounded by a garden containing models of characters from Burns' poems; nearby is the Brig O'Doon over which Tam O'Shanter escaped from witches.

Inveraray Castle, home of the dukes of Argyll, head of the Clan Campbell, is magnificently decorated and has fine grounds leading to the Falls of Aray.

Troon and Prestwick. Further north, however, begin the industrial towns which lead to the workshops and factories of the Clyde.

Out across the Firth of Clyde are the first of the many islands and peninsulas which characterize the deeply indented west coast of Scotland. The nearest of these, reached by steamer from Ardrossan, is the Isle of Arran. This island, with its mountains and hills, fast-running streams, green valleys and pleasant beaches, makes a popular holiday destination. A road runs round the island from Brodick, the island's capital, which is on a bay, guarded by a castle. This castle is the seat of the Dukes of Hamilton, splendidly furnished with Hamilton paintings and other family treasures.

North of Arran is the Island of Bute, close to the Cowal Peninsula and reached by ferry from the mainland. Only 15 miles long by 3 miles wide, Bute is mostly low-lying and covered with farmlands. The popular resort of Rothesay is its capital. Rothesay Castle is Bute's most interesting historical monument and dates back to the 1300s, when it resisted the attacks of Haakon, King of Norway. Later the castle was used as a headquarters for the Stewart kings' operations against the Lords of the Isles who controlled the Hebrides and parts of north-west Scotland. In the sixteenth century the castle was burned down by the Duke of Argyll; it remained a ruin until it was restored in the nineteenth century by the Marquesses of Bute.

To the west of the Cowal Peninsula lies Loch Fyne; a long, narrow loch stretching north to Inverarary, home of the Campbells, Dukes of Argyll. This powerful family, descended from Great Colin of Loch Awe, were masters of the part of Scotland from Loch Linnhe to the Firth of Clyde. As Dr. Johnson discovered on his journey to the Hebrides, Inveraray is an unusual and delightful place. The village and castle were rebuilt in the 1880s and have elegance and style, with white-walled houses around a square by the lochside. The castle is set in marvellous grounds which lead to the Falls of Aray and to Rob Roy's house, a ruined cottage where the bandit was supposed to have lived for some time.

From Inveraray the loch leads south past Lochgilphead, where there is a canal connecting Loch Fyne with the Sound of Jura; and to Tarbert, a fishing port overlooked by a castle, once the residence of Robert the Bruce. Tarbert lies on the isthmus that leads to Kintyre, a long peninsula with Campbeltown on its south-east shore. The journey from Campbeltown to the Mull of Kintyre is about 6 miles, through uninhabited countryside. This is a historic stretch of coast. At Kyle, there are two footprints carved in a rock at the place where St. Columba set foot in Scotland and at the Mull of Kintyre, according to legend, was the spot where the secret of heather ale was lost forever – the last Pict to brew it jumped over the cliff here rather than reveal the recipe to the Scots.

West of the long peninsula of Knapdale and Kintyre lie Jura and Islay, the most southerly islands of the Hebrides. Jura is a rugged place where 5,500 wild deer still roam; Islay is a popular summer holiday resort where the chief local activities are farming and the distilling of malt whisky.

The Central Lowlands

The Central Lowlands of Scotland, stretching from Loch Long to the ancient Kingdom of Fifeshire, are the most populous regions of Scotland and include the two great urban areas of Edinburgh and Glasgow.

Edinburgh, in the county of Lothian, is a beautiful city built on a steep escarpment and the high ground that surrounds it. On the top of the stony ridge running through the city is the castle, approached via the Esplanade, a parade ground where the military tattoos that are a feature of the Edinburgh Festival are performed. The Castle is entered across a moat and through an outer gateway, flanked by statues of Robert the Bruce and William Wallace. The highest part of the castle is King's Bastion where St. Margaret's Chapel, the oldest building in the fortress (c. 1100), is situated. Outside the Chapel is Mons Meg, a cannon built in the fifteenth century which could project an iron cannon ball for over a mile. In the Crown Square, on the lower level, are the Scottish National War Memorial, the Crown Room, Queen Mary's Apartments and the Old Parliament.

From Edinburgh Castle, the Royal Mile – consisting of Lawnmarket, High Street and Canongate – descends to the Palace of Holyrood House, which lies in a park at the base of the crag called Arthur's seat. Holyrood was the scene of the murder of Riccio, secretary to Mary Queen of Scots, and was the headquarters of Bonnie Prince Charlie during his shortlived rule in Scotland.

Before the eighteenth century, fear of attack discouraged the citizens of Edinburgh from living away from the protective environs of the crag, guarded by the castle. However, after the defeat of the Young Pretender in 1745 and the ruthless suppression of the Highlanders, Edinburgh expanded. Trade with England prospered and a new Georgian city arose beyond the loch. The loch itself was filled in to make Princes Street Gardens. The plan for the new broad streets which were to make Edinburgh one of the most elegant cities in Europe was created by James Craig. Robert Adam built the university and part of Charlotte Square. The new Edinburgh attracted many of the outstanding talents of the eighteenth and nineteenth centuries; among them James Boswell, Robert Burns, Sir Walter Scott, Adam Smith, David Hume and Thomas Telford, and the city continues to attract artists, musicians and writers from all over the world to the Edinburgh International Festival which takes place in August every year.

Glasgow, which grew prodigiously during the Industrial Revolution, also began its development in the eighteenth century. It was the departure port for explorers and merchants who were

Below: The historic crag on which Edinburgh Castle stands has been a stronghold since the time of the Picts, changing hands many times in the wars against the English.

Bottom: Sir George Gilbert Scott's Glasgow University building dominates the skyline with its pinnacles and towers.

The elegant Forth Bridge, opened by the Queen in 1964, is 1,818m (6,000ft) long and towers 155m (512ft) above the Forth.

founding communities and trading posts in the new worlds of America, Asia, Africa and the Pacific. As raw materials from all around the globe arrived on the Clyde to be distributed to inland factories, people on Clydebank developed skills at shipbuilding. With the aid of coal and iron mined locally, Clydebank became the world's leading centre for the manufacture of ships' hulls, engines and heavy machinery.

The centre of Glasgow is George Square, where Sir Walter Scott is commemorated by a tall monument, dominating the surrounding buildings. Around the square are the City Chambers, the Merchants' House (home of the Glasgow Chamber of Commerce) and Queen Street Station. Glasgow High Street is to the east of George Square and leads to Cathedral Square. St. Mungo's Cathedral is one of the glories of Glasgow. The building is on two levels, with a lower church of the thirteenth century and an upper church of the fifteenth and sixteenth centuries. The lower church is the tomb of St. Mungo and contains an effigy of Bishop Wischart who crowned Robert the Bruce. The upper church has a fine choir and rood screen.

Other features of Glasgow are the Art Gallery and Museum and Glasgow University, containing the Hunterian Museum. Both lie to the west of Glasgow centre and face the broad, green spaces of Kelvingrove Park. The Art Gallery has a fine collection of the works of Italian, Flemish, Dutch and French painters; the Museum covers armour, engineering, history and natural history. The University, built by Sir Gilbert Scott, has a fascinating collection of anatomical preparations, coins and other items bequeathed by the famous eighteenth century professor of anatomy, Dr. William Hunter.

Across the north of the Central Lowlands lie the foothills of the Highlands. This area of great natural beauty includes the Kilpatrick Hills, and the Campsie Hills along the southern edge of which the Romans built the Antonine Wall. To the east of this green, rolling countryside is the valley of the Forth and its tributary, the Bannock Burn, where Robert the Bruce routed the

English in 1314. Stirling Castle, on its massive crag, dominates the landscape in the green Forth Valley. This impressive fortress was a headquarters of the Scottish kings until James VI of Scotland became James I of England. Mary Queen of Scots was crowned in the fifteenth-century Church of the Holy Rood, situated in the town of Stirling leading to the esplanade and Castle Wynd.

The part of the Central Lowlands north of the Firth of Forth is occupied by the Kingdom of Fife, a region that has always managed to remain separate from the rest of Scotland. The land of Fife is a mixture of farmland and moorland. Along its coasts are small fishing villages, plentiful along the south-eastern shores which curve northwards, round Fife Ness, to St. Andrews. This university town is world-famous for its Royal and Ancient Golf Club, founded in 1754. The Royal and Ancient is the final authority on the rules of the game.

In the centre of Fifeshire is Falkland, whose role as a royal palace complements that of Stirling. At Falkland, courtly manners prevailed and the interior was furnished as a place of leisure. The palace was begun by James IV and completed by James V, who died there after his defeat at Solway Moss. His son, James VI, and granddaughter, Mary Queen of Scots, both resided here and enjoyed the hunting. Later, in 1567, Mary was to return to nearby Loch Leven as a prisoner. After an unhappy 11 months she escaped with the help of George Douglas, the son of Lady Douglas, her warden and taken to Niddry Castle. She was defeated again at Langside, however, and forced to seek refuge further south in England.

The Royal and Ancient Golf Club of St. Andrews was founded in 1754 and has four courses, all of them open to the public.

CASTLES AMONG
—— THE ——
GLENS

G len Mor, known as the Great Glen, which runs from Loch Linnhe on the west coast to the Moray Firth, cuts cleanly through the Highlands of Scotland, separating the mountains of the south from those of the north-west. In the south, the ranges of the Grampian, Cairngorm and Monadhliath mountains are traversed by long rivers that spring from the lochs and mountains of western Scotland; wending their way to the North Sea through green valleys, where salmon leap in tumbling streams and cattle graze along the meadows. Here, although barren mountain peaks and rocky passes add drama to the landscape, there is a good deal of farm land. On the coasts, fishing has long been a major activity, but surpassed today by the wealthy offshore-oil industry. In the eighteenth and nineteenth centuries there was a planned development of new villages in this region of the Highlands; today these communities provide the accommodation and hospitality sought by visitors who tour the Highlands in the summer months, or enjoy winter sports in the Glencoe or Cairngorm areas.

North of the Great Glen the inhabited communities are few and far between, leaving moorland and mountain unspoilt to combine in a natural wonderland with a unique and unforgettable character. In this magical place heather-covered plateaux seem to stretch to infinity and mountains of under 1,525 m (5,000 ft) seem as high as the Himalayas.

On the west coast of this northern region lochs penetrate deeply into the mountains, with little fishing villages clinging like colonies of limpets along the cliff-girt shores. There are great islands such as Skye and Mull; mountainous kingdoms ruled, in medieval times, by the Lords of the Islands – the chieftains of the powerful clans of MacLeod, MacDonald and MacLean. To the north of this wild territory lie the lonely outposts of the Orkney and Shetland Islands – once the ports-of-call for the Vikings. To the west, across the Little and North Minches, are the Outer Hebrides. A frontier with the Atlantic, battered by winter gales, this strange, fragmented strand is also bathed in the warm waters of the Gulf Stream and, like all the north-west Highlands, is a region of mystery and adventure.

These wild rocks are the Storr Hills, which rise to 741m (2,358ft), north of Portree on the Isle of Skye and include the pinnacle called the Old Man of Storr.

South of the Great Glen

Loch Lomond and Loch Katrine are the perfect introduction to the Highlands. They possess, in narrow compass, all the attributes of the land that lies to the north. Entering Loch Lomond from Dumbarton this is not instantly evident, for the southern part of the loch is broad and surrounded by green fields. As you reach the narrow, central section, however, the mountains suddenly press compellingly inwards, with Ben Lomond (173 m; 3,192 ft) standing out challengingly across the loch. At Tarbet the A83 leads off to the west between great craggy mountains, and over a pass steep enough to earn the name of 'Rest and Be Thankful' from those who had to cross it in the days before the motor car. This is the way to Inveraray and the Kintyre Peninsula and, to the north, the mountains of Lorn.

There is no way across Loch Lomond to the east but, if you approach the Highlands through Callander – rightly called the Gateway to the Highlands – you will enter the Trossachs. This is a little world of lochs, pine trees and heather-covered hills, but at weekends too many motor cars destroy the otherwise lovely solitude. Perhaps, therefore, the best way to enter the southern Highlands is via Perth, a noble city on the River Tay praised by Sir Walter Scott in his *Fair Maid of Perth*. Perth has a feeling of spaciousness, with great, open parks, the North and South Inch, stretching along the river. In its centre is St. John's Kirk, the only large building remaining from medieval times. St. John's was badly damaged by the congregation after John Knox preached an inflammatory sermon from its pulpit.

Around North Inch, once a rallying site for the clans as well as a field of clan combat, there are several interesting buildings. Balhousie Castle on North Inch is the Museum of the Black Watch, and the Old Academy, a Georgian building on Rose Terrace, is now used as the county library. Near Perth Bridge is the Art Gallery and Museum which houses an exhibition of relics and memorabilia from Perth's rich past. Down Tay Street, by Queen's Bridge, is the site of Gowrie House, where an unsolved conspiracy to kidnap James VI took place. The Earl of Gowrie and his brother Ruthven were involved in this bizarre affair; the King escaped by summoning aid through an open window and the two conspirators were killed.

From Perth the A9 heads north to the Grampian Mountains, passing some beautiful scenery on the way. It takes you through the narrow valleys of Dunkeld, by the Forest of Dunsinane, to Pitlochry, famous for its drama festival, and the Pass of Killiecrankie. The countryside here provides the first real taste of the Highlands, with pine-covered slopes rising to bare mountain tops. To the south of Pitlochry a road follows the upper course of the River Tay to Loch Tay and the pretty village of Killin with its foaming rapids. To the north, another westbound road leads to Loch Tummel and Loch Rannoch, a region of superb scenery. The road ends at the edge of wild Rannoch Moor, which you can walk across to Glencoe. Continuing north along the main A9 from Pitlochry you come to the narrow wooded pass of Killiecrankie, a lovely place which was once the scene of a battle between the forces of James II and the Scottish highlanders under Graham of Claverhouse.

Beyond the Pass lies the charming village of Blair Atholl, and its elegant castle with white walls and slate-covered turrets.

The Fair City of Perth was the capital of Scotland for a hundred years until 1437, when James I was murdered and the Court moved to Edinburgh.

From Blair Atholl the road goes along Glen Garry to the broad valley of the Spey River, climbing to Aviemore, centre of the Cairngorm region. Here, a cluster of excellent hotels provides every amenity for summer and winter visitors. The Cairngorm mountains are Britain's main winter sports' location and contain some nine peaks, rising to over 1,219 m (4,000 ft). A road takes you into the skiing area and chairlifts do the rest. In summer the area is popular with walkers, canoeists, bird-watchers and all who enjoy outdoor activities. Beyond Aviemore the A9 turns north, out of the Spey Valley, towards Inverness.

Another route from Perth to the north takes you along the coast, past Dundee – now a large industrial city, but with a sprinkling of old buildings at its centre and a castle (closed to the public) on the hills above. From Dundee the road leads across country to the fishing port of Arbroath; the very name of which conjures up the smoky aroma of its famous 'smokies', a type of smoked haddock. In the ruins of Arbroath Abbey you can see the round window in which fires were lit to guide sailors and fishermen home. The town receives many summer visitors, attracted by the sandy beaches and clifftop scenery. Out to sea is Inchcape Rock. Sir Ralph the Rover, a pirate, removed the bell placed on the rock as a warning to shipping, only to be wrecked there himself.

Further along the coast is Montrose, on a peninsula between the sea and the tidal basin formed by the River South Esk. Montrose was once the site of a powerful castle, occupied by Edward I, which was destroyed by William Wallace in the 1300s. Today, only a few old buildings remain in the town; around the church there are still narrow streets and the eighteenth-century Town Hall. Montrose is a popular seaside town; its fine sands and sheltered basin attract bathers and sailors throughout the summer.

Fishing, farming and providing accommodation for summer visitors are the main occupations along this coast of rugged, rocky cliffs and sandy beaches. Near Stonehaven is the beautifully-situated castle of Dunnottar, set solidly on a crag surrounded by sea. The fortress was virtually impregnable and defied the efforts of the Marquis of Montrose to dislodge the Earl Marischal of

The Cairngorms, which lie between the rivers Spey and Dee, rise to over 1,305m (4,296ft) and are a popular skiing ground in winter.

Scotland at the time of the Covenant Wars. During the Civil War it served as a repository for the Scottish Crown Jewels. In 1716 the Jacobite Tenth Earl Marischal of Scotland was obliged to forfeit the estate, which was then broken up and the castle almost destroyed. The ruins of the gatehouse can still be seen; also the drawing room and the Marischal's suite, with its sweeping views of sea and rocks below. The dungeon, called the Whig's Vault, still exists. During the Covenanter troubles 167 men and women were imprisoned there and underwent great hardship. Some tried to escape down the cliffs but few succeeded. Those who were re-captured were executed.

The great city of Aberdeen – once the centre of prosperous cattle and fishing industries, now the oil capital of Britain – lies to the north of Stonehaven. The centre of the city has remained relatively unchanged since the oil boom; especially round the harbour, where fishing trawlers unload tons of fish every day. Marischal Street climbs from the Victoria Dock to Castle Street, a broad, open rectangle in which you will find the Old Town House. This nineteenth-century building has echoes of the old tolbooth, or Guildhall, which once stood on its site. Behind the Old Town House is the Marischal College. Founded in the sixteenth century, it was rebuilt in the nineteenth century in granite, with a pinnacled façade. Opposite, across Broad Street, is one of the new high-rise buildings of Aberdeen, St. Nicholas' House (municipal and tourist offices), dwarfing the Provost Skene's House. Built in 1545, the Provost's House was occupied by the 'Bloody' Duke of Cumberland, who hunted the followers of Bonnie Prince Charlie after the defeat of 1745. It is now a museum. Further down School Hill is the Art Gallery, housing a varied collection of paintings, including works by George Romney and Sir Joshua Reynolds and also nineteenth-century French artists such as Toulouse Lautrec and Monet.

Old Aberdeen, which lies to the north of the city, is a tranquil quarter. King's College (which, with Marischal College, makes up Aberdeen University) and St. Machar's Cathedral are its main features. The cathedral was founded in the twelfth century but the building you see today is mostly fifteenth century. A notable aspect of the interior is the flat, panelled ceiling, decorated with shields of fifteenth-century kings, princes, bishops and nobility of Scotland.

The location of Aberdeen, between the River Don to the north and River Dee to the south, has made the city a meeting-point for routes into the interior of this part of Scotland. The valley of the River Dee, in particular, has long been well-used as a means of communication and, since Queen Victoria bought the Balmoral estate in 1852, it has also become a popular tourist region. Braemar is the main holiday centre. Although its beautiful wooded valley

Arbroath, a busy fishing port and seaside resort, possesses a fine ruined abbey built by William the Lion and dedicated to St. Thomas à Becket.

becomes crowded with spectators at the time of the Royal Braemar Highland Gathering, it is usually a tranquil spot with good hotels and plenty of lovely walks. Downstream is the rebuilt ruin of Braemar Castle, where exciting son et lumière performances are given in summer. The remnants of another castle, Kindrochit, are scattered by the Braemar car park, near the Cluny Bridge.

Further down the river is Balmoral, where the gardens are open to the public when the Royal Family are not in residence. The mock-baronial nineteenth-century castle, set in a beautiful park, stands to the north of the mountain of Lochnagar. More charming still is Abergeldie Castle, a tall, Scottish stone tower in which the future Edward VII lived with his wife, Princess Alexandra. Crathie church, seen in countless New Year television news broadcasts, is nearby.

The holiday town of Ballater is at the meeting place of the Rivers Muick and Dee, amid green woodlands and moors. Highland Games are held here in August (as they are in Aboyne nearer to Aberdeen). From Ballater the Dee flows gently onwards to the sea, through a widening valley where hills and woods give way to more open meadows, and Aberdeen Angus cattle graze.

From Aberdeen the coast continues northwards to Kinnaird's Head and, after the town of Fraserburgh, turns westwards to Elgin and its lovely, ruined cathedral, which has a sad history of pillage and destruction. Founded in the thirteenth century, the cathedral was attacked by the brigand known as 'the Wolf of Badenoch' who set fire to it, and the town, in 1390. It was rebuilt, but later, in 1555, it became the site of a clan battle between the Douglases and the Innes. The cathedral fell into decay and its roof was stripped to pay soldiers' wages. Finally, in 1650, Cromwell's men had their destructive way with what remained. On the brighter side of its story, however, is the devotion given to the ruins by a poor, local shoemaker who was given the title of 'official keeper' in the nineteenth century. His dedication to the work of clearing up the ruins aroused official interest in what remained of the lovely building.

The road leading from Elgin to Inverness passes two infamous and tragic spots, Cawdor Castle and Culloden Moor. Cawdor Castle was the home of Macbeth and his Lady, and was probably where he murdered Duncan (but in an earlier building). Culloden Moor was where Bonnie Prince Charlie's attempt to regain the Scottish throne for his father and the Stuart Kings came to a short and bloody end, bringing the curtain down on centuries of Highland clan life.

Glencoe and the South-west Highlands

Glencoe has a sombre ring to most people's ears for it was here that the MacDonalds were massacred by the Campbells. The tragedy arose because the MacDonald clan had delayed in sending their submission to the government of William III and, consequently, the Campbells were sent in with soldiers to keep them under surveillance. The Campbells lived peacefully among them for several days but the MacDonald's note of submission was being suppressed by the Under-Secretary of State who, it was thought, wanted to make an example of the reluctant clan. The Under-Secretary's actions caused the Campbells to act with, what has seemed to posterity, inexcusable treachery to those who had befriended them.

Glen Coe, where the MacDonalds were massacred, has great scenic splendour with tall, rugged mountains to each side of a fast-running torrent.

Whatever the rights or wrongs of the matter, Glencoe has remained one of the black spots of human behaviour and, during dark winter days, the pass seems full of doom and foreboding. In the bright days of spring, however, when the steep slopes are green and covered in wild flowers, or in the golden days of autumn, it is a glorious place. Great crags rear up on either side and little waterfalls feed the stream which runs down the glen towards Signal Rock, where there is an excellent National Trust for Scotland Visitors' Centre.

At the bottom of the glen is the pretty village of Glencoe, from where a road runs along the southern shore of Loch Leven to Kinlochleven. This town, rather surprisingly, turns out to be a small industrial centre, where aluminium is made. However, the mills of industry are very much overwhelmed by the grandeur of the landscape. There are steep, wooded slopes and sheer summits, which, if you are energetic, you can walk over to the upper Glencoe end of Rannoch Moor.

At the western end of Loch Leven is Ballachulish, where a bridge carries the road from Fort William southwards to Oban and the Cowal peninsula – a most fascinating region of the southern Highlands, full of natural beauty and Highland history. The road takes you south, along Loch Linnhe to Portnacroish and Castle Stalker, perched on a small rock in the centre of a bay. To reach the castle you must take a rowing boat from Port Appin, scene of the murder of Colin Campbell. James Stewart, 'James of the Glens', was hanged at Ballachulish on being found guilty of the murder by a Campbell jury – a story told vividly in Robert Louis Stevenson's

Kidnapped. From Appin the A828 curves around Loch Creran, on the southern shore of which is the Barcaldine Forest. Barcaldine Castle, a tower-like building on the end of the loch, was also the scene of a clan encounter between a Stewart and a Campbell. The Campbell was killed, but returned as a ghost, to predict that his enemy would die at the battle of Ticonderoga – which he duly did.

A little further south, the A828 crosses Loch Etive at the Falls of Lora, one of the many wonders of Loch Etive. These tantalizing falls operate only during the ebb tide, when the waters of the loch pour over the rocks which close the end of the loch from the sea. Over the bridge, on the south side of Loch Etive, the A828 joins the A85 to Oban. To the east, the loch stretches in an L-shape towards the upper Glencoe and Rannoch Moor, where the scenery becomes increasingly breathtaking as you ascend. At Taynuilt, where iron foundries (now museums) made cannons for Nelson, the only ways up the loch are on foot or by boat.

This is the land of Deidre of the Sorrows, who was obliged to leave her home and companions, the sons of Uisneach, to go to Ireland to marry King Conchobar. Finding her listless and un-responsive, Conchobar guessed that it was because she missed her companions. He had them sent for; but only to kill them, in the misguided hope that, with their disappearance, Deidre would forget them. However, his plan was a failure and the unhappy girl slowly pined away and died. Sometimes, the shores of Loch Etive seem full of the sad melancholy of this romantic tale; but the mood soon disappears as you take the Loch Awe road through the striking Pass of Brander, bordered by Ben Cruachan (1,125 m; 3,695 ft).

The scenery around Loch Awe is truly inspiring and, in the centre of the flat, north-eastern shore stands Kilchurn Castle, surrounded by mountains. The castle was built, it is said, by the loving wife of Colin Campbell while he was away at the wars. The loch was a natural boundary for the Campbells of Inveraray against their enemies from the north, and their ruined castles can be seen along the south shore. There is Fincharn, at the south-west end, and Carnasserie on the land that separates Loch Awe from the sea, obliging its waters to flow through the Brander Pass into Loch Etive.

Between Loch Etive and Loch Awe is the land of Nether Lorn – a wild region, roadless except for the A85, which becomes the A816 south of Oban, and winds its way along the coastal plain. Oban, the centre of this world, is a busy port surrounded by hills, protected from the sea of the Firth of Lorn by the island of Kerrera. Though Oban was intended as a fishing port, its real life began when the railway arrived, bringing with it the tourists who fill its hotels and enable its steamers to run profitably on the crossing to the Isle of Mull. The port has many attractions, not least of which is an amusing folly. This was erected by a local banker named McCaig who was so impressed by Rome's Colliseum that he built a replica on the hill above the town. Though regarded with contempt by some, McCaig's Folly has a bizarre charm and pro-vides an interesting foreground to photographs of the harbour. In the town, all the amenities of a resort are provided for visitors who crowd the streets in summer. Outside the town, there is plenty of space for all. On the north shore of the harbour is Dunollie Castle; unfortunately, its crumbling condition makes it unsuitable for visits. Alongside is a perpendicular stone, called the Dog Stone, to which it is said Fingal tied his dog, Bran. To the north, a pleasant, short walk away, is Dunstaffnage Castle, once owned by Robert the Bruce. Dunstaffnage was the scene of a murder at the wedding of Sir James Stewart. He was marrying his common-law wife to ensure that the succession would pass to her son, but was assassinated by the Campbells, husbands of his daughters, in an attempt to prevent this from happening. Although they were too late, for the bond was tied before he died, the Campbells later took the castle by force.

South of Oban the hills of Lorn border the road, and provide many excellent walks along the forest paths. At Loch Melfort, the gardens of Arduine House provide a foretaste of the gardens of Inverewe in the northern Highlands.

North of the Great Glen

From Inverness, the mountains, valleys and lochs of the northern Highlands fan out in a wide arc from Loch Linnhe to Loch Shin. South of this wonderful Highland region lies the Great Glen, a natural fault in the earth's crust containing the longest string of lochs in Scotland. In 1803 Thomas Telford began the construction of the Caledonian Canal which would join Inverness to Fort William, allowing shipping to cross Scotland from the North Sea to the Atlantic and thus facilitating communication and trade between the east and west coasts. This great engineering work, completed in 1822, brought increased commercial activity to the ancient town of Inverness. It became the centre of the Highland wool trade and, in 1855, the terminus of the London, Midland and Scottish Railway which opened up communications with the Highlands and the south.

Before the nineteenth century Inverness had been an important strategic point with a castle, originally a Pictish fort, on Craig Phadrig. It was probably David I of Scotland who built the first stone fort on Castle Hill, and subsequent improvements made the fortress a formidable and much fought-over bastion of the High-

Loch Ness stretches north-east from Fort Augustus, built after the 1715 uprising. The famous monster of the loch 'lives' further up at Urquhart Castle.

lands until it was blown up by Bonnie Prince Charlie in 1745. The castle you see today was built in the nineteenth century on the foundations of the old ruins. Below the castle, on the High Street, is another nineteenth-century building looking older than its years. This is the Gothic Town House, the Town Hall, built in 1878-82, where the first British cabinet meeting held outside London was presided over by Lloyd George. It lies in the busy centre of Inverness, where you will find shops and restaurants and an excellent Highland Tourist Information Office in Church Street.

The River Ness, which flows through Inverness, starts from Loch Ness, to the south-west. This famous home of the elusive monster is a spacious, 24-mile stretch of water, surrounded by wooded hills. The picturesque ruins of Urquhart Castle stand by the water's edge, near to the spot where the monster is supposed to lurk. At the south-western end of Loch Ness is Fort Augustus, where General Wade built a fort in 1729. The fort is now incorporated into a fine Abbey, dating back to the nineteenth century. While at Fort Augustus, General Wade also built several roads to facilitate fast marches with his army; one of these, over the Corrieyarrick Pass to the Spey River, was used by Bonnie Prince Charlie and his army in 1745.

South-west of Fort Augustus, Telford's canal takes boats to Loch Oich, a delightful, small loch. On it shores are the battered ruins of a castle, in the grounds of the Glengarry Castle Hotel. The River Garry enters Loch Oich from lovely, wooded Glen Garry. Loch Oich is joined to Loch Quoich, further west, by the Garry.

From Loch Oich the Caledonian Canal continues to Loch Lochy, into which flows the Arkaig River from Loch Arkaig – another splendid and little-visited stretch of water. From Gairloch lock, at the south-western end of Loch Lochy, there is a magnificent view of Ben Nevis, and a road climbing south-east up the glen brings you to the powerful commando monument at Spean Bridge; from here you can enjoy an even better view of the cliffs of Ben Nevis. Beyond Loch Lochy the Caledonian Canal comes to an end in a series of eight locks, called Neptune's Staircase. They bring boats down to the level of Loch Eil, entering from the west to join Loch Linnhe along the shores of the town of Fort William. The town, stretching along a High Street by the edge of the loch, is on the site of the fort built in 1655 by General Monk. It is a popular tourist centre, providing access to Ben Nevis, and to Loch Shiel, which is where Bonnie Prince Charlie rallied the clans at Glenfinnan and where, today, there is an excellent tourist information office and picnic area.

Loch Shiel is on one of the roads to the Isle of Skye; the other is from Loch Oich, via Loch Loyne and Loch Cluanie, down beautiful Glen Shiel. Glen Shiel is a spectacularly rocky valley, with great boulders and outcrops, which heads down, past the Five Sisters of the Kintail Forest, to Loch Duich, According to legend, the Five Sisters were five girls of Loch Duich who, having waited in vain for their seafaring lovers, were turned into beautiful mountains by a wizard. This delightfully unspoilt region is under the care of the National Trust for Scotland (who provide a Visitors' Centre with audio-visual information at Morvich). The shores of Loch Duich are enchanting. From Inverinate to Dornoch, a minor corniche road provides magnificent views of the loch to the Kyle of Lochalsh, the ferry point for the Isle of Skye and of Eilean Doonan Castle, on its island, at the meeting of Loch Dornoch with Loch Duich.

The Isle of Skye, gesturing like an angry lobster towards the Outer Hebrides, is a place of quite incomparable natural beauty where old traditions are stubbornly preserved – including, in some places, the habit of not taking paying guests on the Sabbath. This is the land of the MacLeods, MacDonalds and MacKinnons; and is the place to which Flora MacDonald brought Bonnie Prince Charlie when he was being pursued by the English on his way to exile in France. The Cuillin Mountains lie to the south of the island, where wild and jagged summits provide challenging terrain for climbers and views of exalting beauty for walkers. Around Dunvegan, home of the MacLeods, whose austere castle stands on a crag at the head of Loch Dunvegan, there are woods – unusual on the otherwise almost treeless Skye. Here also you will find islands where seals gather to breed and, in the past, have given rise to the mermaid legends which abound on this coast. The capital of Skye is the attractive town of Portree, on the east side of the island, which has a fine harbour.

On the mainland, to the north of Skye, lie the beautiful, wild north-west Highlands; with scores of lochs and glorious, empty, mountainous land. Northwards along the coast, between Loch Duich and Loch Broom, some of the most beautiful landscapes in the Highlands can be found. There is Loch Carron, the picture-postcard village of Plockton and the sheer mountains of Loch Torridon. Inland is Benn Eighe (971 m; 3,188 ft) and its nature reserve, and, nearby, Kinlochewe – a favourite centre for open-air holidays. To the west of the village is Loch Maree, among heavily-wooded mountains; Slioch (993 m; 3,260 ft) raises its head at the south-eastern end. At the north-western end of Loch Maree lies Loch Ewe and the extraordinary Inverewe Gardens. The gardens were founded in 1862 by Osgood Mackenzie on the bare but sheltered ground on the north side of the loch. Here, on the same latitude as Siberia, sub-tropical plants are grown thanks to the warm air of the Gulf Stream and the devotion of those who tend the garden.

The north-west of the Highlands is the most sparsely populated region in Britain. There is, however, one charming little town on Loch Broom. This is Ullapool, established in the eighteenth century as a fishing port, it is now a much-frequented centre for visitors who enjoy the unspoilt beauty of this region. Here, fishing boats dock at the pier and also car ferries for Stornoway, on the Isle of Lewis. Occasionally, Russian fishing boats look in at Ullapool, arousing newspaper curiosity.

North of Loch Broom is another superb scenic area. Sheer peaks such as Cul Mor (849 m; 2,787 ft), Canisp (846 m; 2,779 ft) and Suilven (730 m; 2,399 ft) rise out of the marshes and lochs of the Inverpolly National Nature Reserve. A special motor trail, with a one-track, unpaved road, goes around the Reserve to Lochinver, a fishing village with a protected inner harbour. Inland from Lochinver is Loch Assynt, with its ruined Ardvreck Castle, where Montrose was kept prisoner before being taken to Edinburgh for his execution. The ruins are also haunted, it is said, by MacLeod of Assynt's daughter, who married the Devil in order to release her

Ullapool on Loch Broom is a delightful fishing port and holiday resort. At the mouth of the loch lie the lovely Summer Isles, once the home of fishermen.

father from a satanic deal, by which he stood to lose his immortal
soul.

Between Lochinver and the north coast of Scotland are
Eddrachilis Bay, Loch Laxford and Inchard – all beautiful and
lonely places with few habitations. From Durness you can cross
the Kyle of Durness to the west, and take the small bus that
provides an occasional service to the wildest and loneliest headland
in Scotland, Cape Wrath, whose sea-battered cliffs took out across
the Atlantic to Iceland.

The North and East Coasts

At the western end of the north coast of the Highlands are two
magnificent lochs, Loch Eriboll and the Kyle of Tongue. Near the
sea-entrance of Loch Eriboll are the Smoo Caves, a three-
chambered cavern. The Smoo River drops into the inner cave
through an opening made, according to legend, by the Devil
escaping the clutches of the terrible Lord Reay, ruler of this region
of Scotland.

The east side of Loch Eriboll is low-lying; but the east
sea-coast has magnificent cliffs, at the foot of which seal colonies
gather. The Kyle of Tongue, where the pretty village of Tongue is
situated, has historical interest as well as great natural beauty. It
was here that the ship carrying gold for Bonnie Prince Charlie's
troops was forced to seek refuge when pursued by an English
vessel. The crew unloaded the gold and carried it inland to where

Kirkwall, the capital of the Orkneys, is a busy harbour town of narrow streets grouped round the cathedral of St. Magnus, built in 1137 by the nephew of the saint.

the mountains of Ben Hope and Loyal gaze down on Loch Loyal. On hearing that English troops were approaching, they pitched the bullion into the nearest loch. The treasure of Bonnie Prince Charlie has never been found. From Tongue the road winds its way past cliffs and beaches and the valley of Strathnaver – one of the worst-affected by the Clearances in the eighteenth century – to Thurso and John O'Groats. Inland from the coastal road lies a wild country, crossed by few roads. Loch Naver and the small village of Altnaharra are situated near the centre of this wilderness.

Some 30 miles from John O'Groats the road passes the extensive nuclear establishment of Dounreay, where there is an exhibition of nuclear power. Nearby is the village of Reay, headquarters of the Mackay Clan of the northern Highlands. Thurso lies to the east; an important port in the times of the medieval trade between Scotland and the Scandinavian countries, but today a quiet country town. Beyond its bay the land curves to Dunnet Head, the most northerly mainland point in Britain.

Near Duncansby Head lies John O'Groats, a small scattered village, 876 miles from Land's End in Cornwall. From nearby cliffs there are views across the Pentland Firth towards the Orkney and Shetland Islands. From Duncansby Head the coast turns sharply southwards, past Sinclair's Bay to Wick. Wick is a port which, like Ullapool, was rebuilt as part of the plan of the British Fisheries Society to provide work in the Highlands. Today there are still fishing boats in the harbour, and the railway terminus is busy three times a day with the arrival of trains from Inverness. Like all the little villages of the east coast, Wick is a quiet place with lovely clifftop scenery.

At the southern end of the coast road, on the approach to Dornoch Firth, Dunrobin Castle stands on a small plateau overlooking the sea. This was the seat of the Earls of Sutherland and the family still own the nineteenth-century baronial hall which has taken the place of the original castle. The keep in the grounds is part of the original thirteenth-century building. Further south, at the mouth of Dornoch Firth, is the town of Dornoch. The road runs along the north bank of the Firth, crossing it at Bonar Bridge to enter Wester Ross and the rich farmlands of the Black Isle, to the north of Inverness.

Ruined houses on the Isle of Bressay, offshore from Lerwick, in the Shetland Islands, are mute evidence of a struggle for survival that failed.

220

THE EMERALD ISLE
— OF THE —
CELTS

Despite Ireland's rich and tumultuous history, the Irish countryside suggests centuries of idyllic tranquility and peaceful co-existence between man and nature.

Eastern Ireland provides a pastoral landscape of plains and low hills; its character formed by the unremitting toil of generations of farmers who have marked out fields with carefully constructed stone walls and built farms and villages of stone and slate. In the centre the rivers flow amid green meadows; flooding some areas where wild fowl gather and pike, perch and bream breed undisturbed (except for waders and fishermen who enjoy the abundance of food and sport). Two canals cross this central plain, the Royal and the Grand Canals, built in the nineteenth century to provide communications from Dublin to the River Shannon and the east coast. but there are few urban communities in this green and unspoilt land.

In the west the land rises into the mountains; rocky spurs project into the Atlantic and between them is a series of lovely bays, from Bantry to Donegal. The scenery is unforgettably beautiful, bathed in the restlessly changing light of the unpredictable weather, whose stormy moods can quickly change into one of smiling serenity. The soil of the mountain slopes is poor, but good enough to provide grazing for sheep. More fertile ground can be found along the Shannon and its loughs and tributaries.

Though nature rather than history is the main attraction of the Irish countryside, the visitor interested in the evolution of the Irish nation will not be disappointed. On your travels you will find plenty of sites of historic interest. Prehistoric stones are scattered about the western countryside, at Turoe in County Galway for example, or at Roscommon; and there are ancient hillforts in Connacht and Munster, although the remains of the earliest defensive sites are often only mounds and ditches. The buildings, made of wood, have long since disappeared. The later forts however, some of which can be found on the Aran Islands and in County Donegal, were made of stone and their ramparts and towers still remain.

The Cross Slab, also called the Pillar of Riasc, is near the little village of Murreagh on the north side of the Dingle peninsula.

The missionaries too were builders in stone and, with St. Patrick's arrival in the fifth century, there began the building of diminutive stone churches found on the western islands and peninsulas. Near Dingle, the Oratory of Gallarus, a 6×5 m (19½×16½ ft) building shaped like an upturned boat, stands in a field about a mile from the town and there is another tiny stone church in eastern Ireland, at Kells. This is near historic Tara, where St. Patrick founded a monastery and his followers built an eighth-century church called St. Columba's head. The towers which you will often come across in Ireland were also built by monks. These were campaniles to summon the monks to prayers or meals and were also used as refuges from attacks by Viking raiders.

With the coming of the Norsemen there was a hiatus in the development of the Irish countryside but, after the Norman invasion of England and the arrival of Norman lords to settle on Irish land, the building of castles and monasteries was resumed. In the thirteenth century quite sizeable cathedrals began to appear. St. Patrick's and Christ Church in Dublin belong to this period, as do the churches at Limerick, Kilkenny and Killaloe. The Normans encouraged the work of the monks who were able administrators, farmers and traders, and many of the old abbeys destroyed by the Vikings were rebuilt and new ones constructed. The Abbey of the Holy Cross in County Tipperary and Jerpoint Abbey in County Kilkenny are examples of the architecture of this period.

While this development was taking place, the Irish chieftains continued their internecine wars and, as they gradually became more powerful, attracted the attention of the English Kings. Henry II in 1171 and Richard II in 1394 arrived with armies, to protect the interests of their vassal lords. Throughout the Tudor period the struggles between Irish lords continued, and so did the building of castles and fortified manor houses of the type found at Bunratty in County Clare, Clara and Burnchurch in County Kilkenny and Blarney in County Cork. The strong repressive measures taken by Cromwell to bring order and peace to the country, though not immediately successful, did eventually bring an end to the feuding. Thus, in the eighteenth century, the unfortified country houses and town houses which enhance Ireland's cities and countryside today were built.

Dublin and the East Coast

Dublin's Fair City has spread far beyond the boundaries that existed when Molly Malone lived there, and now stretches around Dublin Bay from the Howth Peninsula to the north, to Sorrento Point and Dalkey Island to the south. On the northern peninsula stands the resort of Howth, with its steep streets and harbour, and a sixteenth-century castle to the west of the town. On the southern arm of Dublin Bay is Dun Laoghaire; the terminal for the mail boat from Holyhead, and Ireland's leading yachting centre. To the east, at Sandy Cove, is the Martello tower James Joyce lived in, and which he describes in *Ulysses*.

The centre of Dublin lies along the River Liffey, between the Royal Canal to the north of the city and the Grand Canal to the south. North of the Liffey, west of O'Connell Bridge, lie the Four Courts – the seat of the High Court of Justice of Ireland – in an eighteenth-century complex surmounted by a lantern dome. To the west lies the Custom House. This fine eighteenth-century building by James Gandon has the most impressive of the Dublin

Dublin is a lively mixture of Georgian elegance and twentieth-century commercial and industrial power where the River Liffey meets the sea at Dublin Bay.

waterside façades, with its grand Doric portico and its coppered dome. Today the Custom House is used for government offices. Nearby, in Abbey Street, is the home of the famous Abbey Theatre, source of much of the finest drama of this century including plays by J. M. Synge, Bernard Shaw and Samuel Beckett. On O'Connell Street, which runs north from O'Connell Bridge, is the Gate Theatre, founded by Micheal Mac Liammoir. The Gate Theatre lies on Parnell Square, at the northern end of which is the Municipal Gallery of Modern Art housing, among others, a number of fine paintings of the late nineteenth-century French schools.

The main centre of Dublin lies to the south of the Liffey, and includes its oldest quarter, between Christ Church Cathedral and the castle. Christ Church, extensively remodelled in the nineteenth century, was founded by Silkbeard, a Christian Dane, in 1038.

Only the crypt remains of the original church, but there are large sections of the twelfth-century church built by Strongbow who, it is claimed, is buried in the church – not, however under the tomb claimed for him, as this is topped by a stone carving of a knight who is probably the Earl of Drogheda. When the Church was disestablished in Ireland, the title of cathedral was passed to St. Patrick's Church, to the south of Christ Church on St. Patrick's Street.

The National Protestant Church of Ireland was founded by Archbishop Comyn in 1190 as a rival to Christ Church, and it became a cathedral in the thirteenth century. Owing to its position near the city walls, and the raids of the O'Tooles and O'Byrnes from the Wicklow Mountains, St. Patrick's Church was fortified and its archbishops acquired complete jurisdiction over its lands – a right that lasted until the nineteenth century. By then, however, the cathedral had fallen into ruin and had to be rebuilt. Today, the rebuilt cathedral preserves some of the atmosphere of the thirteenth-century church, though only the Baptistery remains of the original building. For most people the main item of interest is the tomb of one of the past deans, Jonathan Swift, author of *Gulliver's Travels*. He lies in the nave, under the second column on the right, with Esther Johnson, the Stella of his poems, by his side.

To the east of Christ Church, by Cork Hill, is Dublin Castle. It was built by the grandson of Henry I of England and completed by Henry de Londres, Archbishop of Dublin (who also completed Christ Church). The castle can be visited on a guided tour and contains state apartments and a picture gallery.

The east side of Dublin, south of the Liffey, has some fine eighteenth-century public buildings. Among these are the present headquarters of the Bank of Ireland, built in 1729 by E. L. Pearce to house the Irish Parliament, and Trinity College, with its fine Corinthian portico, which is the home of the University of

The gently flowing Blackwater River glides between green banks near the city of Kells, once the site of a famous monastery.

Dublin, founded by Elizabeth I in 1591. Among the students at this renowned centre of learning have been some of the most famous Irish dramatists, writers and statesmen; among them Farquhar, Congreve, Swift, Burke, Goldsmith, Grattan, Wolfe Tone, Carson and Beckett.

Dublin city was, of course, only the centre of a rich area where noble lords and bishops built their palaces and abbeys, so there are many splendid buildings in the countryside surrounding the capital. To the north, near Malahide, lies Malahide Castle. Since Henry II gave Richard Talbot a grant of the land, this was the seat of the Talbots, almost without interruption, until 1975. The castle, although much rebuilt, retains two towers from 1765 and contains a considerable collection of portraits. It was here that the manuscript of *A Tour of the Hebrides* by James Boswell was found, along with a draft of Boswell's *Life of Johnson*. To the north of Malahide is Drogheda, on the River Boyne, near the site of the battle in which William III crushed James II's hopes of regaining the English throne. Nearby is Monasterboice, the ruins of a large religious community founded by St. Boethius. A round tower and the vestiges of two churches with three fine stone crosses in the ground remain.

Inland from Drogheda, along the Boyne Valley, is an important historical and religious area. On the left of the valley rises the hill of Tara. Only earth ramparts and ditches remain of this meeting place of the kings of Ireland. At one time this was the capital of the kings of North Leinster, and a ground plan of the large complex of buildings can still be traced.

To the west lies Kells. A small market town today, Kells was once the site of a powerful monastery which created the beautiful Book of Kells, now in the care of the Trinity College Library. You can see the remains of the monastery called St. Columba's House, a building with a steeply-angled stone roof and a lower barrel-vaulted roof. In the grounds is a round tower and a 3-m (10-ft) high stone cross. Though it survived various Danish attacks, the monastery finally ceased its work after the Dissolution in 1551, and gradually fell into ruin.

To the west of Dublin, in Celbridge, is Castletown House, a fine example of Palladian architecture by Alessandro Galilei. The house consists of a central block and two colonnade wings. Its interior, presently being refurnished, has some interesting features such as the Long Gallery decorated in Pompeian style, and the Print Room.

To the south of Dublin is Enniskerry, a pretty village well-placed for walks in the hills. Beyond is Powerscourt House, in a beautiful location. It is surrounded by an elegant formal garden, as well as natural parkland containing the highest waterfall in the British Isles (120 m; 394 ft). Sadly, the house was gutted by fire in 1974 and all that remains are the granite walls. These are, however, impressive, and from the terrace you can enjoy a marvellous view of the Coley Hills, with the Great Sugar Loaf rising on the southern horizon.

East of the Sugar Loaf is the coast, with its many popular resorts such as Bray and Greystones. Inland are the Wicklow mountains; once the hideout of bandits but now peaceful country-side. Memories of the past are evoked at Glendalough where there are several ruins of churches, including the quaintly-named St. Kevin's Kitchen, a two-storey oratory. The River Slaney flows south from the Wicklow Mountains, through Enniscorthy to

Wexford, a port and manufacturing town where a popular music festival is held each October.

Further west is Waterford, where the waters of the River Barrow, flowing down a green valley west of the Wicklow Mountains meet the Suir, which flows in from the west. Waterford was settled by the Danes in the ninth century and Henry II of England landed here in 1172 and was welcomed by Strongbow. Traditionally the town has been loyal to English kings and, when James II was defeated by William III, it quickly recognized the new monarch. Today, there is not a great deal of evidence of Waterford's medieval past, except for Reginald's Tower on the Quay. There is, however, an eighteenth-century Chamber of Commerce and Church of St. Peter. Now the town is a busy sailing centre and the quay along the Suir is a lively centre of social life. Waterford is universally known for its high-quality glass, which is produced in a factory about a mile and a half from the town, on the Wexford road.

Inland, along the River Suir, is Cahir, once a fortified town, with a massive castle guarding the river crossing. To the north is Cashel, with the Rock of Cashel towering over the town; this was the stronghold of Boru, the great Irish hero of the tenth/eleventh centuries. Before Boru, the rock was occupied by a church built by St. Declan in the seventh century. The cathedral shell you see today was built in the 1300s, but has been much renovated over the centuries. It was badly damaged by a fire caused by the Earl of Kildare in 1495. The Earl, when accused of vandalism by Henry VII, justified it by saying that he thought the archbishop was inside the building! On the south side of the cathedral is Cormac's Chapel, built in the twelfth century by Cormac, King of Desmond and Bishop of Cashel. Below the chapel are the remains of Hore Abbey, a Cistercian building of the 1300s. Cashel also possesses some interesting eighteenth-century buildings, among which are the protestant Cathedral and the Bishop's Palace – now a hotel.

The Ardmore Round Tower, which looks out over Ardmore Bay, was built in the twelfth century as a defence against raiders; nearby are the ruins of the sixth-century oratory and eleventh-century cathedral of St. Declan.

To the south of the Suir river, over the Knockmealdown Mountains, is the valley of the Blackwater – a river that rises in the south-west corner of Ireland and is separated by only a few miles from Killarney and Loch Leane.

The South-west of Ireland

The beauty of Killarney and its lough has been attracting visitors to this part of Ireland since the nineteenth century. Its romantic landscapes aroused the enthusiasm of writers such as Sir Walter Scott and Thackeray; and Sir Julius Benedict was inspired to write an opera entitled *Lily of Killarney*, which was first performed in 1862. Today the attractions of the region are as strong as ever; but you will discover not only beautiful scenery but a gentle pace of life that most people find hard to resist.

The village of Killarney lies on the north side of Lough Leane, on the flat lakeshore through which flow the Rivers Flesk and Deenagh, facing the Sheehy and Tomies mountains to the west. To the west of the village is Kenmare House, home of the Earls of Kenmare. The original building was burned down in 1913 and replaced by a modern house. By the lake's edge is picturesque Ross Castle, with its fourteenth-century keep and its four wall-towers. This castle was once the headquarters of O'Donogue Mor, chief of a section of the O'Donogue clan, but it was surrendered to Cromwell's troops when they mounted an attack by ships from the lake. Further south-east, round the shore of the lake and past another ruined castle, lies Muckross Abbey. Franciscan monks founded the abbey in the fourteenth century and resided there until the Dissolution of the Monasteries under Henry VIII. Of the remains, the most noteworthy features are the tower, the cloisters and the tombs of leading Kerry families such as the O'Donoghues, MacCarthy's, McGillicuddys and O'Sullivans.

All the land on this part of the lake and the hills beyond was presented to the nation in 1932 and contains some of the loveliest countryside around Killarney, in particular the valley joining Lough Leane and Muckross Lake to the Upper Lake. This lies some 9 miles from Killarney, a journey that can be accomplished on a jaunting cart – a horse-drawn vehicle which is appropriate for this lovely and peaceful corner of Ireland. From the Upper Lake a return to Killarney can be made via the Dunloe Gap, on the west side of the park, which is named after the Bourn-Vincents who donated the estate to Ireland. This road passes three small lakes and Kate Kearney's cottage, named after a fair maiden of the nineteenth century who used to provide Irish poteen (illicit whiskey) to passers-by. Today there is a bar which provides legal refreshments to travellers coming and going from the Dunloe Gap.

From Killarney a road connects the indented south-west coast with the sailing and fishing ports of the south coast, and with Ireland's third largest city, Cork. Cork's main street, the Grand Parade, dates back to a period of prosperity when Cork was internationally renowned for its glass-making industry. There are, however, few notable buildings in this avenue, which runs from the south channel of the River Lee into the centre of the city. To most visitors, Cork will be associated with Blarney Castle, which lies some five miles north-west of the city.

Blarney, by the River Martin, is famous for the stone that bestows the gift of the persuasive tongue on those who kiss it. The castle's thick wall and crenellated keep have a sombre air, but this is soon dispelled by the cries and laughter of the hundreds of visitors who arrive in the holiday season to take part in the ritual of kissing the stone – only accessible to those willing to be hung upside-down over the hole in the battlements into which the stone has been embedded.

To the south of Killarney the road runs to Kenmare and then on to Bantry Bay, the most southerly of the big south-western beaches. The small town of Bantry has fine views of the bay and of Whiddy Island, unfortunately spoiled by its oil storage tanks. The best views can be seen from Bantry House and its Italian-style gardens. The house is also worth visiting for its fine furnishing and tapestries. On the north of the bay is Glengariff, a small resort surrounded by wooded valley slopes. Here, the rural beauty of the bay is unimpaired, stretching westwards along the Beara Peninsula, along which run the Caha Mountains. From the north flank of the mountains there is a fine view across the Kenmare River to the Iveragh Peninsula.

The Ring of Kerry is a scenic coast road which runs around the Iveragh Peninsula. It runs from the popular resort of Kenmare, at the head of the Kenmare estuary, to the south of Killarney and the highest mountains in Ireland, the MacGillicuddy Reeks 1,036m (3,414ft) high. On its route, the Ring of Kerry passes Sneem with its brightly painted houses and Waterville, where boats take visitors out to the Skellig Rocks to see the remains of an early monastery. From Waterville the road cuts across the peninsula to Cahirciveen, where it follows the north coast of Iveragh. Along the splendidly scenic road there are extensive views across Dingle Bay to the Dingle Peninsula, the northernmost of the Kerry peninsulas, equal in wild beauty to the Iveragh Peninsula.

On the north side of the Dingle Peninsula are Tralee Bay and the county town of Tralee. St. Brendan was born nearby, at Fenit, 7 miles from Tralee. From Fenit, Tim Severin, the modern

explorer, set off on his journey to prove that Brendan could have crossed the Atlantic. To the north of Tralee lies the Shannon, Ireland's greatest river, which flows along the eastern edge of the province of Connacht.

Ireland's West Country

The country between the course of the Shannon river, which flows down the centre of Ireland, and the Atlantic seaboard is wild, remote and full of strange contrasts. Lakes and bogs prevail along the course of the Shannon and by the Galway loughs, a landscape of flat, reedy land where waterfowl abound. Its streams are full of

There is a 10-mile-long fjord at Killary Harbour in County Galway, which lies between Muilrea Mountain to the north and Ben Gorm to the north.

bream, perch, tench, pike and – above all – trout and salmon. To the west the land rises sharply into barren but beautiful hills, where every change in the weather brings out a new aspect of the landscape. In County Clare the soft, green, southern lowlands rise towards the northern hills. Across Galway Bay is Connemara and the scenic grandeur of the Twelve Ben Mountains. Along the coast the rocky headlands and sand beaches continue north into County Mayo while, around Donegal Bay, lie the coasts of Sligo and Leitrim, counties which stretch inland over hills and mountain outcrops to the flat, wooded lakes of County Roscommon.

Limerick, the city which gave is name to the form of short verse made popular by Edward Lear, is on the River Shannon and is the fourth largest one of the most attractive towns of western Ireland. Well laid-out, with spacious streets and eighteenth-century architecture, Limerick enjoys the advantage of being close to Shannon airport. Once important as the crossing point of the River Shannon, guarded by King John's Castle, Limerick was also, in earlier days, the stronghold of the Kings of Thomond, whose royal palace stood where O'Brien's Castle rises today. Another royal palace belonged to Donal Mor O'Brien, but he gave it to the church and it is now incorporated into St. Mary's Cathedral, standing on the southern bank of the Shannon, opposite King John's Castle.

The fertile valley called the Golden Vale stretches inland from Limerick, and to the north, across the Shannon river, is

Pontoon, near Recess, is an angling resort in County Mayo; green Connemara marble is quarried nearby at Derryclare Lough.

County Clare and Shannon airport. Nearby lies Bunratty Castle, where hearty medieval revelry is provided to entertain modern transatlantic pilgrims nightly. The eastern side of County Clare is relatively demure, with green fields and meadows. The Atlantic seaboard, however, is wild and barren, with dramatic cliffs which reach their highest point at Moher. In the north of the county are the limestone plateaux of the Burren, where the town of Lisdoonvarna dispenses the sulphurous and chalybeate waters whose therapeutic value attracts visitors to the spa.

To the north of County Clare lie Galway Bay and the Aran Islands, a rugged archipelago which provided the setting for J. M. Synge's play, *Riders of the Sea*, and was the inspiration for a classic film, *Man of Aran*. Here the fisherfolk still live traditional, self-sufficient lives. Spinning and weaving are local crafts and the fishermen build their own currachs – boats of laths and tarred canvas.

Galway contains perhaps the most contrasting scenery in Ireland. The vast Lough Carrib, and its low-lying, boggy ground, divide the mountains and rocky seacoast of the west from the limestone plain which stretches to the Shannon river to the east. In the countryside of Galway there is a strong basis of traditional Gaelic culture. Galway City, however, spent much of its medieval life under Anglo-Norman barons who did their best to keep out the wild Irish; as a former inscription on the west gate shows – 'from the fury of the O'Flaherty's, good Lord deliver us'.

In the centre of Galway City lies the Norman church of St. Nicholas where, tradition maintains, Columbus prayed before his journey to America. Nearby is Lynch's Castle, a fourteenth-century manor house. A Spanish influence can be seen in the city and the street called Spanish Parade was once the meeting place of local inhabitants with Spanish traders, who came from across the Bay of Biscay to do business here. Further evidence of the Spanish connection can be seen in the Spanish Arch, and the Browne Doorway in Eyre Square.

To the west lies the wonderful region of Connemara; centred on the popular holiday town of Clifden, set between the Atlantic and the mountains. Along the coast to the north are a number of small, simple fishing villages. Between Galway City and Clifden are the deeply-indented bays of Bertragbhoy, Balconneely, and also Manning Bay where, in 1919, Alcock and Brown made a forced landing after their first transatlantic flight.

The coastal mountains continue into County Mayo, rising to Croagh Patrick (766 m; 2,510 ft) from the shore of Clew Bay, near the fishing town of Westport. On the top of this holy mountain, which rises as an isolated cone above the bay, St. Patrick meditated for 40 days during Lent in 441, with a superb panorama for inspiration. In the bay is Clare Island, home of the redoubtable Grace O'Malley, Queen of the West, who ruled all the Clew coast. She married Mac William Oughter on the condition that either of them could walk free after a year – a period which Grace spent in reinforcing all Mac William's forts with her own troops. On the mainland to the north, in County Mayo, is Carrigahooley Castle, where Grace dismissed her husband after the year's agreement was up.

Off the coast of Mayo is Achill Island joined to the mainland by a bridge, and Mullet which is joined by a narrow isthmus. Both these thinly-populated pieces of land have rocky Atlantic coasts, fretted by wind and sea. Their protected eastern coasts, however, have sandy beaches which are popular with summer visitors. From Bellmullet, on the Mullet Isthmus, a road runs to the north coast of County Mayo, one of the most spectacular seacoasts in Ireland. Headland after headland offer extensive views over the sea and the narrow inlets which provide sheltered waters where visitors can make boat trips under the towering cliffs.

The Northern Region

Donegal occupies the whole of the north-west corner of Ireland and its indented coast, backed by mountains and fringed with sandy beaches, is popular with summer visitors. In the south, near the town of Donegal, lie the resorts of Ballyshannon, Bundoran and Rossnowlagh – all good centres for exploring the region. Inland is Fermanagh, with its extraordinary constellation of little lakes which surround the River Erne as it winds its way through the countryside to the sea at Ballyshannon. Not all of County Fermanagh is low-lying; in the south, on the borders of County Cavan, the Cuilcagh Mountains rise to 660 m (2,188 ft).

Also inland is Lough Derg, in a lonely setting of moor-covered slopes. Here St. Patrick spent 40 days fasting on an island on the lake. The spot was regarded as hallowed ground in the Middle Ages, and Station island is still a popular place for pilgrimages. Today it has two modern churches and a hospice for the pilgrims.

Along the coast to the north is Ardara, at the base of a peninsula. This peninsula separates the bays of Loughros More and Loughros Beg, along the shores of which you can visit many beauty spots with caves, waterfalls and other interesting natural phenomena. This section of the coast, to Bloody Foreland to the north, is a lobster and salmon fishing area where larger quantities of these luxuries are landed than anywhere else in Britain. The coast winds onwards, past resorts and fishing villages, to Lough Swilly and the Innishowen Peninsula. Innishowen is to the west of Lough Foyle, at the southern end of which lies the city of Derry.

Derry is an ancient town, founded in the sixth century by St. Columba who built a monastery there. Since its early days, Derry has had to fight off invaders. First came the Norseman and then the Normans, who failed to establish a foothold on Lough Foyle. In the seventeenth century, however, a large number of Protestants arrived and built town walls. These are still in good condition and are now part of the walk around the town. In 1669 the famous Siege of Derry took place. Jacobite forces blocked the entrance to the River Foyle and Protestants were besieged in the town for 105 days without food or drink. The siege was broken when a ship, *The Mountjoy*, forced its way through the boom erected by the Jacobites. Some of the cannons used in the siege still stand on the city ramparts.

To the south of Derry the Sperrin Mountains rise up, along the borders of County Tyrone; and to the east lies County Antrim,

Carrickfergus Castle, which stands on a rock by the harbour, was built in 1180 by John de Courcy, and is one of the finest castles in Ireland.

The Giant's Causeway in County Antrim is one of the wonders of the geological world, probably first brought to the world's attention by Dr. W. Hamilton in 1786.

the north-east corner of Ireland which is separated from Scotland, at Tor Head, by a channel only 13 miles wide.

Along the north coast of Derry and Antrim a limestone plateau drops in sheer cliffs to the sea. This is a beautiful place and between the resorts of Portrush and Ballycastle many sandy bays can be found. There are also dramatic outcrops of rock – none more so that the Giant's Causeway, an extraordinary rock palace of hexagonal basalt columns, formed when hot lava burst out onto the earth's surface in the Cainozoic period. It was near the Giant's Causeway that one of the ships of the Spanish Armada, *Girona*, sank in 1588. Nearly 400 years later its treasures have been salvaged, and they can now be seen in Belfast's Ulster Museum.

A long spine of hills runs down the east side of Antrim. Rivers run off the watershed to the east, forming the Nine Glens of

Antrim. The glens vary in size and shape, but all open out into the North Channel which separates Ireland from Scotland. Among the best known are Glenariff, which has waterfalls and woods in its upper course and a wide valley, bordered by rocky outcrops, as it nears the sea; Glenarm, which has a seventeenth-century castle amid its woods; and Glencoy, a small glen with several cascades in its stream which flows into Carnlough, where there is a good, sandy beach.

At the southern end of County Antrim is the city of Belfast, built on the site of a fort that commanded the River Lagan. During the Anglo–Norman occupation of Ireland, a series of castles built on this site were fought over by the O'Neills of Tyrone and the English. The matter was settled when the Earl of Essex seized and murdered Brian O'Neill during a banquet in the castle in 1574. This was the end of O'Neill power in Belfast and, during the next 50 years, the O'Neill followers were gradually eliminated and Belfast was settled by English and Scottish immigrants. In the seventeenth century a new life began for Belfast when the Earl of Stafford encouraged the development of the linen trade. Later, in the eighteenth century, there began the shipbuilding industry which made Belfast's shipyards famous throughout the world as builders of great ocean liners, including the ill-fated Titanic.

The centre of Belfast is Donegal Square where the City Hall stands on the site of the old White Linen Hall. Around the square are a number of centres of learning, including the Linenhall Library and, in College Square, the College of Technology and the Royal Belfast Academical Institution. To the east of the city, near the River Lagan, are the Royal Courts of Justice. To the south of the city is the Botanic Gardens Park, adjoining Queens University. The Ulster Museum lies to the south of the gardens and contains five different departments, including an Art Museum with a particularly fine collection of watercolours and drawings, and the treasures salvaged from the Spanish Armada's *Girona* in 1968.

Belfast is the industrial and political capital of Northern Ireland, renowned for its ship-building, aircraft manufacture and linen mills.

Belfast is particularly well endowed with open spaces and parks. Among those are Bellevue, to the north, where there is a zoological garden and Belfast Castle, home of the Earl of Shaftesbury; and Stormont Park, 5 miles east of the city centre, where the Parliament Building stands on a fine, wooded site.

To the south of Belfast is County Down, a fertile countryside of green hills, rising to the granite heights of the bewitching Mountains of Mourne in the south. To the east lies Strangford Lough, a vast, almost land-locked expanse of water, where a large part of the shore is now a wildlife and bird reserve.

Inland from Belfast, in County Tyrone, is another vast area of low-lying land around Lough Neagh, but to the west are the hills and mountains of that beautiful area of countryside which lies at the heart of Ulster.

The beautiful mountains of Mourne lie to the south of Belfast, behind Newcastle, with their highest point at Slieve Donard (847m; 2,796ft).

INDEX

page numbers in italics refer to illustrations

239